SOPHIA VANCE

Homemade
HEALTHY
DOG FOOD
2 IN 1 GUIDE + COOKBOOK

Whip Up Tasty and Nutritious Meals for Your Furry Friend With Fast and Easy Recipes: Give Your Dog the Best With Many Mouthwatering Treats

TABLE OF CONTENTS 🐕

Introduction 7

Chapter 1: Becoming a Home Chef for Your Dog 8

Choice of Ingredients 8

Meats and Proteins 8

Seafood 9

Fruits 10

Vegetables 11

Grains 12

Herbs 12

Prohibited Foods 14

Meat Meal 14

Chocolate 14

Melamine 14

Butylated Hydroxyanisole 14

Onions, Chives, and Garlic 14

Macadamia Nuts 14

Corn Syrup 14

Avocado 15

Xylitol 15

Alcohol 15

Cooked Bones 15

Why Rotation Is Important 16

What to Do and What to Avoid 17

Mistakes With Homemade Dog Food 17

Preparing a Nutritionally Unbalanced Recipe 17

Not Adding Essential Nutrients to the Food 18

Using Unsafe Ingredients 18

Not Cooking the Food Properly 18

Chapter 2: Nutritional Guidelines..19

   Nutritional Properties of Ingredients...19

      Protein...19

      Fats..19

      Vitamins...19

      Fiber...20

      Carbohydrates...20

      Minerals...20

   Nutritional Supplements...21

      Easily Digestible Foods for Dogs..21

Chapter 3: Homemade Dog Food Diets..23

   What Homemade Dog Food Diets Are Available?............................23

      Raw Feeding Diet...23

      Vegetarian Diet..23

      Dry or Wet Food..23

      Grain-Free Diet..24

   Pros and Cons of Major Diets for Dogs...24

   What Should Be in a Balanced Diet?..25

      Healthy Fats...25

      Carbohydrates...25

      Meat..26

      Organ Meat..26

      Vitamins and Minerals..26

      Fiber...26

      Superfoods...26

Chapter 4: Guidelines to Feed Your Dog...27

   How Often Should You Feed Your Dog?...29

   Testimonials...29

      Testimonial #1...29

      Testimonial #2...30

      Testimonial #3...30

      Testimonial #4...30

Chapter 5: How to Store Homemade Dog Food 31

Chapter 6: Homemade Dog Food Recipes...32

  Twenty Main Dish Recipes for Dogs 32

    chicken and spinach for puppies 32

    Turkey and Vegetables for Puppies 34

    Puppy Food With Quinoa, Pasta, or Millet..35

    Chicken and Vegetable Stew 36

    Beef Stew 38

    Chicken Balls for Dogs...39

    Dog Food With Beef and Vegetables 40

    Vegan Dog Food With Rice and Quinoa 42

    Vegan Dog Food With Rice and Lentils..43

    Vegetarian Food for Puppies and Dogs 44

    Grain-Free Dog Food...45

    Chicken Casserole for Senior Dogs..46

    Stew for Diabetic Dogs...48

    Beef and Vegetables for Diabetic Dogs...50

    Diabetic Dog Food With Vitamin Therapy for Dogs Requiring Insulin 51

    Grain-Free Beef and Vegetable Meal for Diabetic Dogs 53

    Food for Dogs With Diarrhea and Upset Stomach......................................54

    Healthy Homemade Dog Food 55

    Chicken and Quinoa Soup 56

    Chicken Soup 57

    Raw Food Cakes 58

    Low-Carb, High-Protein Dog Food 61

  Savory Treats 63

    Diabetic Dog Treat 63

    Peanut Butter and Pumpkin Dog Treats 64

    Cheddar Dog Treats 65

    Chicken Dog Treats 66

    Chicken Jerky...67

    Bacon Dog Treats 68

Carrot and Oats Treat 69

Basic Dog Biscuits 70

Vegan Dog Biscuits..72

Chicken, Rice, and Cheese Dog Treat 73

Homemade Kibble 74

Chicken and Vegetable Kibble 74

Multigrain Kibble 75

Nutty Pumpkin Kibble 77

Apple and Vegetable Kibble 79

Crunchy Kibble..81

Dry Dog Food With Beef and Vegetables..83

Dry Vegan Dog Food 85

Dry Dog Food With Turkey and Vegetables 87

Sweet Treats 88

Peanut Butter Pupcakes 88

Blueberry Doggy Muffins 90

Frosty Peanut Butter Popsicles 91

Strawberry and Banana Dog Ice Cream 92

Peanut Butter and Banana Ice Cream 93

Meals and Pastries for Special Occasions..94

Rabbit Meal 94

Beef Stew 95

Shepherd's Pie for Dogs 96

Dog Birthday Cake 97

Mini Pumpkin Pie 99

Chapter 7: Imperial and Metric Conversion Chart 101

....101

Conclusion 102

References...103

Image References...104

INTRODUCTION

Nothing can bring you more joy than a lively, healthy dog in your home. However, that is only possible if you take care of your dog as best as possible. This includes everything from getting him to exercise enough to eating well. Good nutrition is the most important aspect of keeping your dog healthy and free from illness. A healthy diet will help your dog live a long, happy life beside you.

In the same way, you need to eat healthy, quality food to stay fit; so does your dog. The problem is that they are not as discriminating about eating and would joyfully gobble up anything offered. However, the responsibility of ensuring that your dog is being fed nutritionally balanced meals is on the dog owner. A lot of the healthy foods that are recommended for humans are also good for dogs. There are also many foods that you need to completely cut off from their diet to keep them healthy.

If you don't know the right foods and what foods must be prohibited from your dog's diet, this guide will help answer all your questions. Following these simple guidelines will help you select the most nutritious food for your dog and prepare healthy, delicious meals at home. Every health-conscious person knows that processed food harms the body more than good. This applies to humans as well as dogs.

Processed foods are convenient but tend to contain many additives and preservatives that are harmful in the long run. So stop feeding your dog from those processed bags of dog food and prepare healthy, homemade meals instead. Any experienced dog owner will tell you that dogs stay healthier with meals prepared at home.

Use this book as a guide to learn about the nutritional requirements of dogs through various ages and what ingredients you need to feed them. Do a little meal prep and try the numerous recipes here. They aren't a lot of work, and your dog will love you all the more for it. The biggest benefit? You can help your favorite companion be healthy and stay by your side for many years.

CHAPTER 1: BECOMING A HOME CHEF FOR YOUR DOG

Let's begin with the basics of becoming a home chef for your dog. Dogs have their own list of foods that are healthy and unhealthy for them. For instance, you might not have known that garlic is bad for dogs. This section will help you learn about choosing the right ingredients for cooking home-cooked meals for your dog. You will learn about certain prohibited foods that should never be included in their diet. You also learn about some mistakes many home chefs make, but you can avoid them.

Choice of Ingredients

The first step is to pick out the right ingredients to make healthy food for your dog at home. The nutrients from the food you feed your dog will help them grow well and maintain a healthy metabolism. However, not all ingredients are made the same. If you want to choose the most nutritionally beneficial ingredients for your dog, pick from the following list.

Meats and Proteins

- *Beef.* It is a high-quality protein and amino acid source. It should be fed in moderation due to its high cholesterol content.

- *Deboned chicken.* It is an affordable lean protein source but unsuitable for dogs with chicken allergies.

- *Deboned turkey.* It is a lean protein source with fewer calories than chicken.

- *Lamb.* It is a good protein source with complex amino acids but is high in cholesterol and trans fat. Overweight dogs should not be fed lamb meat.

- *Deboned duck.* It is a high-protein meat with vitamins B3 and A. It contains a lot of fat and sodium.

- *Rabbit.* It is a lean protein source with fewer calories than chicken.

- *Pork.* It is a palatable protein source that needs to be cooked thoroughly to avoid parasitic infections.

- *Venison.* It is a lean protein source that contains vitamin B. It is high in cholesterol and trans fat.

- *Eggs.* Eggs are a good source of potassium, iron, and calcium. They are also the easiest source of adding protein to your dog's diet. However, feed eggs in moderate quantities to avoid high cholesterol.

- *Raw bones.* Raw bones are a good source of glucosamine, calcium, and other minerals. They should ideally be ground up first and then added to your dog's meals.

- *Liver.* Liver can be taken from chickens, cows, and some other animals. It contains nutrients like vitamin A, phosphorus, iron, and selenium. Feed it in small amounts to avoid excess consumption of vitamin A.

Seafood

- *Salmon.* It is a lean protein fish that contains omega fatty acids. Dogs with pancreatitis cannot be fed salmon.

- *Anchovies.* It is an affordable protein fish that has a good amount of omega fatty acids.

- *Herring.* It provides omega fatty acids but is high in sodium content.

- *Sardines.* It is a nutrient-dense source of protein that is high in sodium.

- *Crustaceans.* They are rich in nutrients and proteins like potassium, glucosamine, and magnesium and should be cooked.

- *Fish oil.* Fish oil is a good source of omega fatty acids and increases energy levels.

Fruits

- *Apples.* Apples provide vitamins A, C, and fiber. The seeds need to be removed before feeding to your dogs.

- *Blueberries.* They are a good source of antioxidants and help in controlling cholesterol levels.

- *Pumpkin.* It contains vitamin C, potassium, fiber, and beta-carotene, which help improve overall health.

- *Cranberries.* They are a good source of antioxidants but must be consumed in moderation.

- *Banana.* This soft yellow fruit is a favorite among dogs and is a better alternative to other fatty treats they may enjoy. Bananas are a good fiber, potassium, and vitamin C and B6 source. Always remove the peel since it can cause digestive issues.

- *Cantaloupe.* This sweet melon is a good source of fiber, vitamin A, folate, vitamin C, niacin, and vitamin B6. It adds flavor to dog food, but the seeds and rind should be removed. Dogs with diabetes should not be given too much of this fruit since it is high in natural sugars.

- *Mango.* Mangoes are rich in vitamin C, vitamin E, vitamin B6, and fiber. They should only be given in small amounts since overeating can cause diarrhea.

- *Pear.* Pears are a good source of vitamin A and vitamin C. The seeds are dangerous for dogs and should be removed first. Dogs with diabetes should not be given pears since the natural sugar content is high.

Vegetables

- *Sweet potatoes.* Sweet potatoes are a very common ingredient used in commercial dog food. It's a rich source of fiber and complex carbs.

- *Carrots.* Carrots can be fed raw or cooked to dogs and are a good source of beta-carotene that promotes ocular health.

- *Celery.* Celery is rich in magnesium, potassium, and other vitamins. It is low in calories and good for dogs with overweight issues. It also promotes good dental health.

- *Alfalfa.* These leafy greens are a good source of protein, fiber, and various minerals and vitamins. Alfalfa should only be fed in small quantities since it can cause stomach pain.

- *Chicory root.* Chicory root can be fed as a vegetable, or the inulin can be extracted. It works as a prebiotic and promotes good gut health.

- *Zucchini.* Zucchini is high in fiber and very low in calories.

- *Seaweed.* Seaweed comes in various forms, but powdered kelp is easily available. It is rich in iron, magnesium, calcium, and many minerals. Dogs with thyroid issues should not be fed seaweed due to the iodine levels.

- *Spinach.* Spinach is rich in vitamins and is very fibrous. It can be fed raw or cooked to dogs but only in moderation due to the high oxalic acid content. Excess consumption of oxalic acid can lead to kidney problems.

- *Peas.* Peas are a good source of vitamins C, K, and B1. They boost immunity and help in improving blood circulation.

- *Broccoli.* Broccoli is a great source of minerals and vitamins. The florets should be consumed in small quantities since too much can cause gastric distress.

- *Asparagus.* Asparagus is high in fiber content and helps in regular bowel movements for dogs. However, it adds a bad odor to their urine.

- *Wheatgrass.* Wheatgrass is packed with nutrients and can be served raw or as juice. It provides beneficial enzymes, but the strong smell may not appeal to your dog.

- *Brussels sprouts.* They are high in antioxidants and are good for blood circulation. Brussels sprouts contain many minerals and vitamins, but the isothiocyanate levels are high. Excess consumption can cause gas or diarrhea.

Grains

- *Brown rice.* Brown rice is a healthy carbohydrate that contains iron, omega-3 oils, and magnesium. Ensure it is cooked well before you serve it to your dog.

- *Wheat germ.* Wheat germ is a low-gluten option that contains many vitamins. However, it should not be given to dogs with allergies.

- *Millet.* This gluten-free grain is a good option for dogs with food allergies. It is a good source of potassium, iron, and B vitamins. It is also very easy to digest.

- *Rye.* Rye is a whole grain that is rich in nutrients and vitamins. It is a complex carbohydrate that lowers high blood sugar levels. However, it should not be fed to dogs with food allergies.

- *Barley.* It is a fibrous grain that is a good source of copper and selenium. This grain retains its nutrients even after cooking but should be avoided if your dog has celiac disease.

- *Brewer's yeast.* It is a type of living fungus that is good for gut health and is a source of B vitamins.

- *Lentils.* These legumes are highly nutritious and are a great source of iron. They help regulate levels of blood sugar. However, lentils may cause stomach irritation in dogs with sensitive systems because of their tough skin.

- *Rice bran.* Rice bran is obtained from the outer layer of grains of rice. The high amount of fiber is good for digestion and a good source of magnesium, B vitamins, and omega-3 oils.

- *Flaxseed.* Flaxseed can be added as a whole ingredient, or the oil can be extracted and used. It is a great omega fatty acid source that improves your dog's coat and skin texture.

Herbs

- *Parsley.* This flavorful herb is filled with vitamins and also has anti-inflammatory properties. Dogs with kidney issues should not be fed with parsley.

- *Turmeric.* Turmeric works as a natural anti-inflammatory agent and also has antioxidants.

- *Rosemary.* This aromatic herb has antioxidant properties that benefit your dog. However, it should be given in small quantities.

- *Green tea.* Green tea provides antioxidants that can improve the overall health of your dog. However, it should be given in small amounts due to the caffeine content.

Prohibited Foods

Some foods are very harmful to dogs and should be avoided as much as possible. Avoid including these in your dog's meals to avoid health issues.

Meat Meal

Leftover meat scraps are rendered to remove fat. Meat meal is unhealthy for dogs.

Chocolate

A stimulant called theobromine in chocolate makes it toxic for dogs. It can lead to kidney failure if your dog eats too much chocolate.

Melamine

It is a filler ingredient to increase the protein content in dog food. Melamine is plastic that contains nitrogen and is harmful to dogs. Consuming this ingredient can lead to kidney failure.

Butylated Hydroxyanisole

Butylated hydroxyanisole (BHA) is a chemical preservative that extends the shelf life of oils and fats. Small quantities of it are generally not harmful to humans, but too much of it can affect the liver and kidneys of your dog.

Onions, Chives, and Garlic

Any food from the onion family can lead to red blood cell damage and gastrointestinal irritation. The signs of toxicity are usually visible a few days after consuming these foods.

Macadamia Nuts

A toxin in these nuts is known to cause weakness and swelling in the muscles of dogs. It also causes panting and affects the nervous system.

Corn Syrup

Most dog treats or dog food sold in the market contain corn syrup. It is a concentrated sweetener that has a very high glycemic index. Eating foods with corn syrup will cause your dog's blood sugar levels to rise alarmingly and put them at risk for health issues like obesity and diabetes. Corn syrup or foods with corn syrup should ideally be eliminated from their diet.

Avocado

Persin is a compound in avocado plants' fruits, seeds, and leaves. It causes diarrhea and vomiting if consumed by dogs.

Xylitol

Xylitol is an artificial sweetener that is present in many sugar-free or diet products. Consuming any food with xylitol can cause your dog to suffer from hypoglycemia and may lead to liver failure.

Alcohol

Alcohol causes intoxication and diarrhea and may even damage the nervous system if consumed by dogs. It is dangerous even if your dog consumes a small dose of it.

Cooked Bones

Many people assume that cooking the bones makes them safer for consumption by dogs. However, it causes the bones to harden, and the splinters can cause perforation if your dog eats these bones. A raw uncooked bone is much safer for dogs.

Why Rotation Is Important

Rotation feeding is the practice of rotating the homemade meals that you feed your dog. It would mean switching up the proteins or giving them dry food instead of wet food for a while. Many dog owners have adopted this feeding method instead of giving their dogs the same food their whole lives.

Rotation feeding has many benefits for your dog. Like humans, dogs need a variety of nutrients too. Feeding them the same food for too long can cause a deficiency of nutrients that might not be present in the particular meal you are currently feeding them. The most obvious benefit of rotation feeding is that it keeps mealtime exciting for them. Dogs love to eat, and eating the same meal for too long can get monotonous.

Rotation feeding helps deal with food allergies and is also great for their digestive system. Often, dogs develop food allergies when they are fed the same protein for too long. This constant exposure can result in allergic symptoms like itchy skin or an upset stomach. It happens because their immune system develops an adverse reaction to that protein over time.

With rotation feeding, you give your dog different proteins, which can help prevent such food allergies from developing. It also promotes better digestive health. The presence of good bacteria in their gut aids in digestion. Feeding the same meal daily can limit the healthy bacteria in their digestive tract. By having more variety in the diet, your dog gets exposed to better bacteria for their gut too. This, in turn, helps their digestive system function a lot better. This is why rotation feeding has become quite popular among dog owners.

You can use the recipes in this book to prepare different meals for your dog and practice rotation feeding. It helps to improve and maintain the overall health of your dog. It is very easy to get started with rotation feeding. For instance, you can feed them dry food for a week and switch to wet food or raw food the next.

Switching up the protein source in their meals is the most important part of this method. A simple way of doing this is feeding them different types of meat or fish each time. If you prepare their meals with chicken for a week, try using turkey the next week. As you keep rotating their meals, you will notice your dog gets healthier and benefits from the nutritionally balanced diet you feed them.

What to Do and What to Avoid

1. Don't substitute ingredients without checking with a vet. The ingredients in most dog food recipes are tried and tested. If you want to substitute them, you may throw the nutritional ratio off balance in the recipe.

2. Don't try too many diets. Many dog owners try various diets for their dogs, assuming these would benefit their health. However, experts say that multiple diets can have a negative effect on your dog's health. They are also more likely to cause nutritional deficiencies in your dog's diet.

3. Don't rely on random sources. There is a lot of information out there, but not all are reliable. Not every diet is healthy for your dog, and not every recipe is balanced. This is why you should never look up or follow unreliable sources online or even in books. Look for information from trusted experts who know what is good for your dog's health. The local board-certified veterinarian is a much better source than an online forum where anyone can post anything.

4. Do monitor their health and dietary changes over time. Pay attention to your dog's weight, overall health, and dietary changes. Keep track of their medical history. Monitoring all this can make a lot of difference in promoting good health and longevity.

5. Do prepare a balanced diet. Your dog needs a balanced diet as well. If you don't prepare balanced meals for them, it can cause nutritional deficiencies or even toxicity from excess consumption of a particular food. The lack of a balanced diet can cause malnutrition and have a detrimental effect on your dog's health.

Mistakes With Homemade Dog Food

Cooking for your dog allows you to care better for them. However, there are many mistakes that you might end up making if you aren't careful too.

Preparing a Nutritionally Unbalanced Recipe

The food you prepare needs to meet the unique nutrient requirements of your dog. These nutrients have to be in specific ratios to be balanced. The amount of protein, fats, and carbohydrates needs to be balanced. So does the ratio of other vitamins and minerals in the food. This is why you need to check the recipe first to ensure that it meets your dog's nutritional requirements.

Not Adding Essential Nutrients to the Food

Any homemade dog food should always include ingredients that will include essential nutrients. For instance, you can add ground-up bones to include calcium to their diet. Many people also forget to add fiber to their dog's food, and this affects their digestion.

Using Unsafe Ingredients

It is important to learn about all the harmful foods for dogs. A common list is provided in this book, but you also need to pay attention to any specific food allergies your dog has. Avoid including such ingredients in their meals. Giving your dog some of your chocolate may be tempting, but it can be fatal for them.

Not Cooking the Food Properly

Some dog food can be given raw, but other recipes need to be prepared by cooking. Cooked food is generally a lot safer for consumption. If the food is uncooked, there is a risk of bacterial growth or nutritional imbalances. This is why it is important to follow the instructions and always cook homemade meals well before giving them

to your dog.

CHAPTER 2: NUTRITIONAL GUIDELINES

There are about 40 essential nutrients that must be included in your dog's diet. All these nutrients play a role in ensuring good health for your dog. If you don't prepare meals with these nutritional requirements in mind, it negatively affects your health. Inadequate nutrition prevents optimal functioning in their body and causes illness and suffering.

Similarly, excess amounts of certain nutrients may also lead to disease. Many dog owners don't notice the symptoms of such issues until it is too late. The symptoms are usually mild initially but escalate into a serious issue that may be fatal for your dog later. To avoid this, consider nutritional guidelines recommended for your dog throughout its life span.

Nutritional Properties of Ingredients

Protein

The protein in a dog's diet should include essential amino acids which their bodies cannot produce. These 10 amino acids are required to create glucose which the dogs need for energy. Chicken, turkey, salmon, whitefish, etc., are good sources of this nutritional element.

Fats

Fats and fatty acids are added through animal fats and plant seed oils in homemade dog food. The fatty acids are needed for cell structure support. They also help in keeping your dog's coat and skin healthy. Fats are also an ingredient that improves the taste of homemade food. Plant-based oils like flaxseed, canola, soybean, etc., are good sources.

Vitamins

Vitamins are essential for good growth and maintenance. A lack of vitamins can lead to deficiencies, but excessive amounts can also cause toxicity. Dogs need vitamins A, D, E, K, and

B. These are obtained from leafy greens, fruits, vegetables, fish, and plant oils. They also need choline obtained from egg yolks, fish, and liver.

Fiber

Fiber is needed to promote better gastrointestinal system functions. Adding fiber to dog food helps prevent obesity. Carrots, brown rice, apples, etc., are good sources.

Carbohydrates

Carbohydrates are needed for energy. They include dietary fibers, sugars, and starches. Rice, oatmeal, and quinoa are good sources.

Minerals

Dogs need 12 essential minerals. They are as follows:

- Calcium, which can be obtained from tofu, green beans, and cauliflower, helps to keep bones and teeth strong.

- Phosphorus, which can be found in eggs and meat, helps maintain stronger teeth and bones.

- Magnesium, sodium, potassium, and chlorine from whole grains, fruits, and vegetables help in cell signaling and muscle contraction.

- Iron from poultry and red meat helps improve immunity and support red blood cells.

- Sulfur from fish, meat, and molasses helps improve the quality of your dog's fur, skin, and nails.

- Selenium from seafood, meat, and vegetables helps boost immunity.

- Iodine from dairy and seafood is good for their thyroid.

- Copper from seeds and whole grains supports bone growth.

- Zinc from eggs, liver, and lamb helps support healthy skin and boosts immunity.

Nutritional Supplements

- glucosamine
- chondroitin
- taurine
- methylsulfonylmethane (MSM)
- mannan oligosaccharides (MOS)
- beet pulp
- yucca extract
- calcium and phosphorus
- tapioca starch

Easily Digestible Foods for Dogs

Dogs, like humans, can suffer from food allergies, sensitivities, and other issues. Only 14–33% of dogs have food allergies (Giovanelli, 2020). Common signs of these food sensitivities or allergies in dogs include itchy skin, hyperactivity, diarrhea, vomiting, or weight loss. The cause is usually genetic, but the environment can also play a role. However, if you can identify such issues, it gets easier to avoid feeding your dog anything that will cause such reactions. So what and how do you feed dogs with these dietary restrictions?

First, try an elimination diet to determine which foods will potentially lead to a reaction. You will have to feed them that particular ingredient and nothing else to determine the actual allergens. Once you do this, just eliminate the foods which cause adverse reactions.

Next, most food sensitivities, allergies, and gastrointestinal problems are caused by proteins or carbohydrates. Primarily, you might notice them react to dairy products, beef, chicken eggs, corn, soy, or wheat. In this case, you can try to feed them other novel protein sources like salmon, duck, venison, or buffalo meat. Since most dogs are not exposed to these foods before, they are also less likely to have an adverse reaction. Some vets also recommend the hydrolyzed protein diet for canines with these issues. This diet requires your dog to eat proteins broken into multiple small amino acids. If your dog eats the proteins in such small parts, their body will generally not recognize the protein and thus not have an allergic reaction.

The best thing to do is avoid commercial pet foods for your dog if they suffer from such problems. Cooking homemade meals for your dog with nutritious ingredients and eliminating the allergens will help keep them healthy. It might also help to feed your dog smaller meals multiple times a day instead of a couple of large meals. Eating too much at once may make it more difficult for their body to digest the food. However, remember to add all the major food groups to their diet, even if you have to substitute certain ingredients.

For instance, if your dog is allergic to wheat or corn, you can still give them brown rice or barley for a portion of carbohydrates. Also, try adding probiotics to their diet to aid with digestion. Probiotics are also known to help dogs with food allergies. Adding a little yogurt to their food is a good step. You can also ask the veterinarian to recommend some probiotic supplement that is safe for consumption.

In general, dog allergies are quite common and not something to worry about if you can manage them well. As long as you can identify the foods that cause the adverse reactions, feeding your dog other healthy foods is easy.

CHAPTER 3: HOMEMADE DOG FOOD DIETS

Let's discuss dog food diets. Like there are various diets for humans, there seem to be many diets for dogs. However, it is important to check with the vet before you put your dog on a specific diet. This section will help you learn about various dog food diets with their pros and cons. It will also help you learn how to create a balanced diet for your dog while cooking homemade meals.

What Homemade Dog Food Diets Are Available?

The following are some dog food diets you may have heard of:

Raw Feeding Diet

In this diet, dogs are fed only raw ingredients. Their meals are not cooked, and the ingredients are frozen or freeze-dried. Before feeding time, the food is defrosted and given raw. Usually, raw diets consist of bones, meat, and offal without cooking.

Vegetarian Diet

Some vegans or vegetarians also choose to feed their dogs a vegetarian diet. This means they won't be given any animal products and hence no meat. It may seem like an oxymoron, but many people choose to put their dogs on a vegetarian diet these days. Dog owners are usually concerned about eating meat or other ethical reasons. It may be due to medical issues for some dogs, and the vet may recommend a vegetarian diet.

Dry or Wet Food

Vets may sometimes recommend that a dog only be given dry or wet food. This is often done when the dog has a medical condition that makes consuming a particular food consistency difficult. In other cases, combining dry and wet food in your dog's diet is best.

Grain-Free Diet

Many dog owners also try the grain-free diet, which doesn't include grains in their dog's meals. Hence, anything like wheat, rice, or corn is eliminated from the diet. This diet usually benefits Irish setters since they tend to develop celiac disease and need to avoid gluten. The grain-free diet can also be adapted to help diabetic or obese dogs reduce their carbohydrate intake.

Pros and Cons of Major Diets for Dogs

One of the major benefits of making a home-cooked diet is that it allows you to custom-make food according to your dog's health status and dietary preferences. You can use fresh and good-quality ingredients that are generally easy to source. You don't have to feed them any commercial food that contains hidden ingredients that may be potentially harmful. It also allows you to ensure that all their nutritional needs are being met.

There are some cons when it comes to certain home-cooked diets as well. For one, it requires time to prepare the food. There is also variable quality control. Another con to consider is that commercial dog food may be more affordable, while home-cooked meals require a higher investment depending on the quality of ingredients. It can be difficult to follow a home-cooked diet for your dog if you don't know much about its nutritional requirements either.

A home-cooked diet is only ideal if the meals give your dog all the nutrition and calories they need. For instance, a vegetarian diet is not the best choice unless your dog's medical status requires it. Dogs are omnivores, and being on a plant-based diet may make it difficult to ensure they get the protein they usually obtain from meat. A plant-based diet with too much fiber can be difficult for dogs to digest. Feeding your dog a diet with only meat or plant-based food can cause nutritional deficiencies.

The con associated with the grain-free diet is that grains are an important source of energy for dogs. Unless your dog suffers from gastrointestinal or skin issues caused by grain consumption, removing grains completely from its diet would not be beneficial. While the amount of grains in the diet needs to be monitored to avoid weight gain, it is better to include at least a portion of some grains in your dog's meals daily.

What Should Be in a Balanced Diet?

A balanced diet plan is required when you intend to prepare all your dog's meals at home. It can be a little complex to figure out their nutritional needs, but it gets easier with time.

Healthy Fats

Healthy fats for dogs include omega-3 fatty acids and omega-6 fatty acids. Fats provide more concentrated energy than proteins or carbohydrates for your dog. The fats added to their diet should always be from high-quality ingredients and be easy to digest. Coconut oil, animal fat, and poultry fat are good sources of healthy fat for dogs.

Carbohydrates

Dogs benefit from grains, vegetables, and fruits just like they do from meat. Adding these to the dog's diet will provide them with essential minerals, vitamins, and fiber. Pumpkin, rice, squash, and berries are healthy carbohydrate sources for dogs.

Meat

Meat is essential for healthy growth for dogs. It is a good source of protein to promote immunity, cell growth, organ maintenance, and hormone balance. Good sources of animal-based proteins include chicken, lamb, and beef. The essential amino acids in meat provide your dog with a lot of nutrition.

Organ Meat

For dogs, organ meat is just as beneficial as other animal meat. The liver, kidneys, and heart of animals like chicken and beef are good for dogs. Livers are a good source of fat-soluble vitamins A, E, D, and K. Kidneys are a great source of protein and folate. Heart meat is a good source of taurine, iron, selenium, zinc, and vitamin B.

Vitamins and Minerals

Ingredients that contain vitamins A, D, E, B, and K and trace minerals like iron and zinc gluconate are recommended. If you pick natural ingredients with these vitamins and minerals, your dog won't need any extra supplements and can avoid deficiencies.

Fiber

Fiber is one of the most important parts of a dog's diet because it helps in promoting better gastrointestinal function. Include both soluble fibers as well as insoluble fibers. Insoluble fiber can be obtained from grains to help increase the dog's fecal bulk. Soluble fiber helps in preventing constipation and allows water retention. Fruits like blueberries and plants are some good sources of soluble fiber.

Superfoods

Foods like blueberries, quinoa, kale, and chia seeds are called superfoods. They contain high amounts of beneficial compounds like fiber and antioxidants. Adding these ingredients to your dog's food makes it much healthier.

CHAPTER 4: GUIDELINES TO FEED YOUR DOG

The nutritional requirements of your dog will vary according to many factors. This includes their breed, activity level, age, medical history, environment, and current health condition. These markers can help you determine the amount of food you need to feed them. Feeding your dog every time he wags his tail or looks at you with those puppy eyes can be tempting. However, overeating can be a real cause of many health issues for dogs. On the other hand, not feeding them enough will also affect their health and stunt proper growth. So how much do you feed your dog?

The best choice is to go to the vet and ask what the ideal amount of food is according to your dog's breed, age, weight, etc. They can help you calculate a more appropriate feeding routine accordingly. You will also have to understand that the amount of food your dog needs will depend on how active they are. A lazy dog does not need as much food as a dog that never sits still. An active dog should be given a little extra food to allow for the amount of energy they spend throughout the day.

Here is a tool to help you calculate your dog's caloric needs during a particular life stage (The Ohio State University, n.d.):

Resting energy requirements (RER) = Body weight of the dog in kilograms raised to the ¾ power by 70

The RER is the first that needs to be met. This is the amount of energy your dog needs to perform all their essential body functions.

If your dog is a 10-kilogram adult dog, their RER would be 70(10)^¾ or 400 calories daily. The following chart can help you calculate the caloric needs using RER in different stages of your dog's life:

Neutered adult dog	1.6 x RER
Intact adult dog	1.8 x RER
Inactive dog	1.2–1.4 x RER
Weight loss	1.0 x RER for the ideal weight
Weight gain Active dog	1.2–1.8 x RER for the ideal weight 2.0–5.0 x RER
Puppy (0–4 months)	3.0 x RER
Puppy (>4 months)	2.0 x RER

Here is another tool to help you understand the usual feeding guidelines for dogs:

The following chart can help you determine the portion of food to give your dog based on caloric needs. To measure, use an 8-ounce cup. The general guidelines are to feed about ⅓ cup of food for every 10 pounds over 100 pounds of body weight. Since puppies are at the growing stage, they need almost double the feeding amount recommended for adults. When a dog is pregnant or nursing, it is better to opt for free-choice feeding.

	Dog weight	**Cups per day**
Toy dog	3 lb	⅓ cup (139 calories)
	6 lb	½ cup (233 calories)
Small dog	10 lb	¾ cup (342 calories)
	15 lb	1 cup (464 calories)
	20 lb	1 ½ cups (576 calories)
Medium dog	30 lb	1 ¾ cups (781 calories)
	40 lb	2 ¼ cups (969 calories)
	50 lb	2 ⅔ cups (1,145 calories)

Large dog	60 lb	3 cups (1,313 calories)
	70 lb	3 ½ cups (1,474 calories)
	80 lb	3 ¼ cups (1,629 calories)
	90 lb	4 ¼ cups (1,779 calories)
	100 lb	4 ½ cups (1,926 calories)

How Often Should You Feed Your Dog?

Dogs love to eat, regardless of their breed, age, etc. They want to eat all the time. However, responsible dog owners would only let their dogs eat as much as they need. It may be difficult to say no to those puppy eyes, but it is the only way to keep them healthy. It is recommended to feed your dog twice a day. You can ask your vet for guidance if your dog may need a little extra or reduced feeding. For instance, when dogs become overweight or their activity levels are low, some dog owners only feed them once daily. However, avoid doing this for puppies since they need more nutrition for growth.

You can try free-choice feeding for your dogs when they are pregnant or nursing. This means you would leave out the entire amount of food recommended for that day in their bowl. Your dog is then free to go eat whenever they feel hungry. They may nibble on it a bit at a time throughout the day or even eat it all at once. However, it is best to time their meals if they are not pregnant or nursing. Feed them once in the morning and once later in the evening. Leaving too much food out at once will only make them overeat.

Testimonials

The following testimonials were taken from Dr. Joglekar, a veterinarian, and pet owners about their experiences on feeding their dogs home-cooked meals (n.d.):

Testimonial #1

I have a wonderful 8-year-old German shepherd named Steffi, and taking care of her has become ever so simple since I started preparing her meals at home. Long gone are the days when I depended on store-bought kibble and snacks or treats to care for her nutritional needs. One day, after an intense discussion with the vet, I was introduced to the world of home cooking for dogs. Over the last six months, Steffi managed to shed a couple extra pounds and achieve her ideal weight goal, she is more energetic than before, and her coat seems extra shiny too. So, I think home-cooked dog food is a great way to improve your pet's health.

Testimonial #2

We are repeatedly told that home-cooked meals are better than eating fast food. I thought it was time to apply the same logic to my dog's diet. My 5-year-old golden retriever was always a fussy eater. He would only eat a specific type of kibble and nothing else. However, he is certainly fond of all treats and snacks. After a lot of research, I decided to go for the home-cooked dog food route to see the results for myself. My dog loved this change! He enjoys mealtimes now. Also, I feel much better knowing that I am feeding my furry companion home-cooked meals devoid of harmful additives and preservatives.

Testimonial #3

As a vet, I have treated and handled countless pets, especially dogs. A common concern most pet parents have is whether their dog is getting the needed nutrients from store-bought dog food. They also worry about whether most of the snacks and treats on the market are good for their pooch. Well, one simple secret that I believe actually helps dogs is home-cooked dog food. Yes, they have different nutritional and dietary requirements, but learning about them is simple. Also, giving your dog home-cooked dog food and treats ensures pet parents are more in control of their dog's diet, helps feed fussy eaters, makes it easier to avoid allergens, and strengthens the bond between the pet parent and their dogs.

Testimonial #4

As a responsible pet owner, taking care of your pet's nutritional needs is your responsibility. I understand this quite well because I have been feeding my furry friend only home-cooked dog food, snacks, and treats since he was a pup. I never gave him any store-bought kibble. Now, I can see the different benefits my 3-year-old husky gets from home-cooked food. His coat seems to be quite shiny, he has barely any teeth issues, and he is more energetic than other dogs his age. This is more than enough motivation for me to keep going and stick to the homemade dog food diet for my pet. Another wonderful benefit of feeding my dog home-cooked pet food is giving me more opportunities to bond with him.

CHAPTER 5: HOW TO STORE HOMEMADE DOG FOOD

Once you choose the right ingredients and start preparing homemade dog food, you also need to know how to safely store the food to keep it fresh. Safe storage will help prevent spoilage, contamination, mold, etc., and help the food last much longer. The following tips will help you store homemade dog food properly:

- Always keep wet food and dry food separately. Wet food should always be stored in the refrigerator. While serving your dog with this wet food, make sure it doesn't sit in their food dish for too long. The longer wet food is exposed to air, the easier it degrades.

- Only cook a two-to-three-day batch of food at once. Any cooked food should be stored in containers in the refrigerator or freezer until consumed. Avoid exposing the prepared food to too much heat or moisture.

- Don't keep any bags of dog food on the floor because it can get contaminated more easily. It also makes it easy for your dog to access when they aren't supposed to be eating.

- Get separate containers for storing dog food. There are specially designed containers that are more appropriate for storing dog food. They are usually pet-proofed and make it difficult for your pet to get to them. These containers are available in different sizes as well.

- Always store the food away from your pet. Dogs tend to overeat even when their meals are done. If you store the food within easy access, they can usually find a way to get into it. They might also spill the food while trying to do this and cause wastage. Store the food in spots where it will be safely out of reach.

- Don't mix old batches of food with new batches. The older the food, the higher the risk of contamination or spoilage. Mixing freshly prepared dog food with old food will only cause more waste. It can even cause your dog to fall sick if you don't notice the small amounts of spoiled food mixed in.

- Store the food away from direct sunlight. Exposure to direct sunlight can elevate the food's temperature and increase humidity levels. Both these factors increase the risk of food spoilage.

- While buying ingredients, always check or pay attention to the expiry dates. Use up the food that is closer to the expiry date soon. Keep these toward the front so you can use them faster.

CHAPTER 6: HOMEMADE DOG FOOD RECIPES

Twenty Main Dish Recipes for Dogs

CHICKEN AND SPINACH FOR PUPPIES

Quantity produced: About 3 lb **Preparation time:** 10 minutes **Cooking time:** 40–45 minutes	**Nutritional values for 1.5 oz:** *Calories: 65* *Fat: 2.8 g* *Carbohydrate: 4 g* *Protein: 5.8 g*

Ingredients:

- 2 lb ground chicken
- ½ can (from 15 oz can) tomato sauce
- 1 medium yam
- ¾ cup dried brown rice
- 2–3 cups fresh spinach
- ½ tbsp olive oil

Directions:

1. Follow the directions given on the package and cook the brown rice.

2. Prick the yam with a fork at several places and place it in the microwave. Cook for 6–7 minutes on high heat or until it turns tender. Turn the yam for about 3–4 minutes through cooking.

3. Place a pot over medium heat and pour oil in it. Add chicken once the oil is hot and stir until the chicken is well cooked. As you stir, break the meat into smaller chunks.

4. Mix well with brown rice, yam, tomato sauce, and spinach. Turn off the heat.

5. Blend the mixture with an immersion blender until chopped into smaller pieces. Do not make it very smooth.

6. After cooling for an hour, transfer the mixture into a bowl and keep it covered in the refrigerator for 8–9 hours.

7. Line parchment paper on a baking sheet. Make balls of the mixture, about 1.5 oz each, and place them on the baking sheet.

8. Freeze until firm. Transfer the balls into freezer-safe bags (keep enough for a week in each bag). Seal the bags. You can keep one bag in the refrigerator and freeze the remaining bags.

9. Thaw a bag in the refrigerator all night. Warm the required number of balls and serve.

TURKEY AND VEGETABLES FOR PUPPIES

Quantity produced: About 2 ½ lb **Preparation time:** 10 minutes **Cooking time:** 40–45 minutes	**Nutritional values for 1.5 oz:** *Calories: 66* *Fat: 2.5 g* *Carbohydrate: 4.8 g* *Protein: 6.13 g*

Ingredients:

- 1 ½ lb ground turkey
- 1 carrot, peeled, shredded
- ¼ cup fresh or frozen peas
- ¾ cup dried brown rice
- 2 cups fresh spinach
- ½ medium zucchini, shredded
- ½ tbsp olive oil

Directions:

1. Follow the directions given on the package and cook the brown rice.

2. Place a stockpot over medium heat and pour oil in it. Add turkey and stir often until the meat is brown. As you stir, break the meat into smaller pieces.

3. Turn off the heat. Mix well with brown rice, carrots, zucchini, peas, and spinach. Cook until the vegetables become tender. Turn off the heat.

4. Serve as much as required and store the remaining in an airtight container in the refrigerator. You can also store in freezer-safe bags, enough for one week in a bag.

PUPPY FOOD WITH QUINOA, PASTA, OR MILLET

Quantity produced: Around 2 lb **Preparation time:** 10 minutes **Cooking time:** 35–40 minutes	**Nutritional values for 3 oz:** *Calories: 124* *Fat: 5.9 g* *Carbohydrate: 7.3 g* *Protein: 11.3 g*

Ingredients:

- 1 ½ lb ground turkey or any other meat of choice
- ½ carrot, peeled, shredded
- ¼ cup pumpkin puree
- ½ apple, cored, chopped
- ½ medium zucchini, peeled, shredded
- ½ squash, peeled, deseeded, grated
- ½ cup dried quinoa, whole-grain pasta, millet, or any other whole grain of choice
- 2 tbsp coconut oil or coconut flakes
- ½ tbsp olive oil

Directions:

1. Cook the grain following the directions given on the package. Add extra water if using quinoa, or cook for a couple of minutes longer for pasta or other whole grain than the time mentioned on the package, as we want soft grain for the pup.

2. Pour oil into a pan and place it over medium heat. Add turkey and stir often until the meat is brown. Stir continuously to break the meat into smaller chunks. Once the meat is cooked, drain off excess fat from the pot.

3. Add carrot, pumpkin puree, apple, zucchini, squash, cooked quinoa, and oil.

4. Turn off the heat. Let it cool down and serve. Store the remaining food in an airtight container in the refrigerator or freezer. It is better to store portions in the freezer so that it is easier to thaw and serve.

CHICKEN AND VEGETABLE STEW

Quantity produced: About 5–7 lb **Preparation time:** 15 minutes **Cooking time:** 3 hours	**Nutritional values for 6.5 oz:** *Calories: 236* *Fat: 6.7 g* *Carbohydrate: 17.4 g* *Protein: 25.57 g*

Ingredients:

- ½ lb antibiotic-free chicken livers, chopped
- 2 lb boneless chicken breasts, chopped into chunks
- 1 lb lean ground turkey (optional)
- 1 cup uncooked brown rice
- 1 can (15 oz) of black beans, drained, rinsed
- 1 can (15 oz) of kidney beans drained, rinsed
- 2 small sweet potatoes, peeled, cubed
- 2 uncooked stew bones
- 1 cup frozen peas
- 1 large carrot, peeled, cubed
- 2 large eggs

Directions:

1. To make bone broth, add bones into a pot of water (about 3 qt).

2. Place the pot over high heat. Let it boil for about 1–1 ½ hours.

3. Discard the bones and use only the broth.

4. While the broth is boiling, cook the turkey if using. Place the turkey into a skillet and cook until brown. As you stir, break the meat into smaller pieces.

5. Transfer the meat to the pot of stock. Add chicken, black beans, kidney beans, chicken livers, brown rice, sweet potatoes, carrots, and peas, and place the pot over high heat. Stir occasionally.

6. When it starts boiling, turn down the heat and simmer until the rice is cooked and very soft and the meat and vegetables are cooked.

7. Crack and whisk eggs in a bowl. Pour the egg into the stew and mix well.

8. Cook it all for 15 more minutes, while stirring occasionally.

9. Place some of the stew (for about 3–4 days) in an airtight container in the refrigerator. Store the remaining stew in small freezer-safe bags as per portion in the freezer.

BEEF STEW

Quantity produced: About 6–7 lb Preparation time: 10 minutes Cooking time: 50–60 minutes	Nutritional values for 3.8 oz: *Calories: 125* *Fat: 1.8 g* *Carbohydrate: 16.1 g* *Protein: 11.02 g*

Ingredients:

- 5 cups water
- 2 cups white or light brown rice
- 4 cups sweet potato, cubed
- 4 cups blueberries
- 5 lb sirloin, chuck roast, or ground beef
- ½ cup rolled oats
- 4 cups chopped green beans
- 2 cups green peas

Directions:

1. Add water, rice, sweet potato, blueberries, meat, rolled oats, green beans, and green peas into a large pot.

2. Place the pot over high heat. When the mixture starts boiling, turn down the heat and cook until the meat and rice are cooked. Let it completely cool down and serve it to your dog.

3. Store some of it in an airtight container in the refrigerator. Store the remaining in freezer-safe containers or bags in the freezer.

4. Mix an equal quantity of stew and kibbles in a bowl and serve it to your doggy.

CHICKEN BALLS FOR DOGS

Quantity produced: 5 lb Preparation time: 30 minutes Cooking time: 30 minutes	Nutritional values for 2 oz: *Calories: 180* *Fat: 11.4 g* *Carbohydrate: 10.7 g* *Protein: 7.9 g*

Ingredients:

- 8 cups cooked rice
- ½ cup cornmeal
- ⅔ cup chicken broth
- ⅔ cup chopped parsley
- 10 cups cooked chicken, chopped
- 4 tbsp flaxseed oil
- 2 large carrots, peeled, shredded

Directions:

1. You can use any rice, brown or white. Cook the rice following the directions given on the package.

2. Measure out 8 cups of cooked rice and add into the food processor. Also, add cornmeal, broth, parsley, chicken, flaxseed oil, and carrots and process until well combined.

3. Do not process until very smooth.

4. Transfer the mixture to a bowl and cover it in the refrigerator for 2–3 hours.

5. Place parchment paper on a baking tray. Make balls of the mixture, 2 oz each, and place them on the baking sheet.

6. Freeze until firm. Transfer the balls into freezer-safe bags (keep enough for a week in each bag). Seal the bags. You can keep one bag in the refrigerator and freeze the remaining bags.

7. Warm them up before serving.

DOG FOOD WITH BEEF AND VEGETABLES

Quantity produced: Around 3 lb **Preparation time:** 15 minutes **Cooking time:** 50–60 minutes	**Nutritional values for 16 oz without bones, without serving options):** *Calories: 846* *Fat: 27 g* *Carbohydrate: 107 g* *Protein: 43 g*

Ingredients:

- 1 lb ground beef
- 2 cups uncooked brown rice
- ½ tbsp chopped fresh rosemary
- ½ can (from 13.5 oz can) of spinach, drained
- 1 cup canned pumpkin puree
- 3 cups water or more if required
- ½ lb assorted beef bones
- ½ can (from 15 oz can) of sliced carrots, drained
- 3 eggs

To serve (optional)
- cooked oatmeal
- cooked barley

Directions:

1. Place a skillet over medium-high heat. Add beef and cook until brown. As you stir, break the meat into smaller crumbles. Discard extra cooked fat from the skillet. Remove from heat.

2. Combine water and brown rice in a stockpot. Transfer the browned beef, rosemary, and beef bones and place the pot over high heat.

3. When the water starts boiling, reduce the heat to medium-low and cook until the rice is very soft and is breaking down. Stir on and off. Add more water if required. The consistency should be thick. Turn off the heat.

4. Add carrots and spinach into a blender. Crack the eggs into the blender. Add the eggshells as well. Blend until smooth.

5. Pour the mixture into the pot of rice. Also, add pumpkin and stir until well incorporated.

6. Cover the pot and let it rest for 5 minutes. Uncover and let it cool down. Serve it to your furry baby when ready.

7. Store leftover food in an airtight container and refrigerate until use. It can last for 4–5 days.

8. To serve, you can serve only the dog food, add some cooked oatmeal or barley, and serve warm. Serve at least a piece of bone at each time.

VEGAN DOG FOOD WITH RICE AND QUINOA

Quantity produced: About 2 lb **Preparation time:** 10 minutes **Cooking time:** 30 minutes	**Nutritional values for 14.5 oz:** *Calories: 559* *Fat: 18.7 g* *Carbohydrate: 85.7 g* *Protein: 17.3 g*

Ingredients:

- 1 cup cooked quinoa
- 1 cup cooked brown rice
- 1 cup drained, cooked, or canned lentils, chickpeas, or black beans
- ¼ cup nutritional yeast
- ½ can pumpkin
- ¼ cup green peas
- ½ cup cooked squash
- ½ cup dried cranberries or Craisins
- ¼ cup roasted nuts of your choice (like peanuts, cashews, walnuts, etc.)
- 1 cup chopped greens of your choice (like spinach, radish greens, beet greens, etc.)
- ¼ cup natural nut butter of your choice
- ⅛ cup flaxseeds
- ½ cup corn
- ½ cup edamame
- ½ cup unsweetened applesauce
- ½ bag of frozen leftover healthy bits (optional)

Directions:

1. Add quinoa, brown rice, chickpeas, nutritional yeast, pumpkin, green peas, squash, cranberries, nuts, greens, nut butter, flaxseeds, corn, edamame, and applesauce into the pot and place it over medium heat.

2. Leftover healthy bits are anything leftover that is vegan and your pet eats. Add these if desired. Mix well.

3. Cook until the vegetables are tender, stirring often. Turn off the heat.

4. Let it cool down and serve as much as required. Store the remaining food in an airtight container in the refrigerator or in freezer-safe bags in the freezer. Make sure to store one or two portions in each freezer-safe bag. Thaw overnight in the refrigerator. Warm it up and serve.

VEGAN DOG FOOD WITH RICE AND LENTILS

Quantity produced: About 3–3 ½ lb Preparation time: 10 minutes Cooking time: 45 minutes	Nutritional values for 9 oz: *Calories: 250* *Fat: 7.9 g* *Carbohydrate: 37.2 g* *Protein: 10.1 g*

Ingredients:

- ½ cup uncooked brown rice
- ¾ cup cooked or canned chickpeas
- ¼ cup dry lentils
- ¾ cup cooked or canned great northern navy beans (for dogs under 7 years) or ½ cup oats (for dogs more than 7 years)
- ½ lb frozen peas, thawed
- ½ lb frozen cauliflower or broccoli florets
- ½ lb frozen spinach, do not thaw
- ½ lb frozen green beans, thawed
- ½ lb carrots, peeled, shredded
- ¼ cup ground flaxseeds
- ¼ cup chia seeds
- 3 ½ cups water
- ¾ cup cooked sweet potatoes, cubed
- ½ can (from 15 oz can) of pumpkin

Directions:

1. Place chickpeas and great northern beans in the food processor and give short pulses until roughly chopped.
2. Transfer the beans to a pot. Add rice, oats, lentils, broccoli, peas, spinach, green beans, and water and stir.
3. Place the pot over high heat. Lower the heat and cook until the rice and lentils are soft when the mixture starts boiling.
4. Stir in chia seeds and flaxseeds. Add pumpkin and sweet potato and mix well. Let it cool down and serve it to your pet.
5. Divide the remaining food into portion-size bags or containers and freeze.

Note: You can use an instant pot or pressure cooker for this recipe if you have it handy.

VEGETARIAN FOOD FOR PUPPIES AND DOGS

Quantity produced: About 4 lb **Preparation time:** 10 minutes **Cooking time:** 20 minutes	**Nutritional values for 4 oz:** *Calories: 98* *Fat: 1.4 g* *Carbohydrate: 16.4 g* *Protein: 4.9 g*

Ingredients:

- 4 cups cooked or canned black beans
- 1 cup fresh spinach, chopped
- 1 large apple, cored, chopped
- 1 medium zucchini, chopped
- ½ cup low-fat cream cheese
- 2 cups dry quinoa
- 1 cup chopped butternut squash
- 1 large pear, cored, chopped
- 3 cups plain yogurt

Directions:

1. Follow the directions given on the package of quinoa and cook the quinoa.

2. Transfer the quinoa to a bowl. Mix well with black beans, spinach, apple, zucchini, cream cheese, butternut squash, pear, and yogurt.

3. When it cools down, you can serve your little darling as much as required. Store the remaining in the refrigerator in an airtight container. It can last for about 3 days.

4. This is good for diabetic dogs as well.

GRAIN-FREE DOG FOOD

Quantity produced: About 1 ¼ lb **Preparation time:** 20 minutes **Cooking time:** 30 minutes	**Nutritional values for 1 cup:** *Calories: 291* *Fat: 12 g* *Carbohydrate: 7 g* *Protein: 37 g*

Ingredients:

- 2 medium carrots, peeled, chopped
- ⅛ cup water
- 1 ½ lb ground chicken
- 1 ½ tbsp sunflower oil
- 3 eggs
- 3 oz chicken livers, chopped
- 2 cups baby spinach leaves
- 1 apple, peeled, cored, and chopped

Directions:

1. Beat the eggs in a bowl but do not discard the shells.

2. Preheat the oven to 350 °F. Place eggshells in the oven and bake for 5–7 minutes or until dry.

3. Once baked, crush them thoroughly.

4. Add apples, carrots, and water to a pot. Place the pot over high heat. When it starts boiling, turn down the heat and cook covered until carrots and apples are soft. Turn off the heat. Mash the mixture, if desired, to the desired texture.

5. Place a skillet over medium heat. Add chicken livers, ground chicken, crushed eggshells, beaten egg, and oil into the skillet and stir well. Stir occasionally. Cook until the chicken is brown and the chicken livers are not pink. As you stir, break the ground chicken into smaller crumbles.

6. Scatter spinach on top and keep the skillet covered. Cook until the spinach is soft.

7. Turn off the heat. Add apple mixture and mix well.

8. Serve as much as required and place the remaining food in an airtight container. Keep the container refrigerated. It can last for 3–4 days.

9. Place a cup of the mixture in a microwave-safe bowl. Heat until warm and serve.

CHICKEN CASSEROLE FOR SENIOR DOGS

Quantity produced: About 3 lb **Preparation time:** 15 minutes **Cooking time:** 50–60 minutes	**Nutritional values for 12 oz:** *Calories: 649* *Fat: 21.7 g* *Carbohydrate: 57.2 g* *Protein: 53.7 g*

Ingredients:

- 2 boneless chicken breasts with skin on
- ½ cup cabbage, chopped
- ¼ cup green beans, chopped
- ¼ cup spinach, chopped
- 1 tbsp olive oil
- ¼ cup carrots, peeled, sliced
- ½ cup small broccoli florets
- ¾ cup brown rice

Directions:

1. Pour 2 inches of water into a pot and place the pot over high heat and place a steamer basket in it.

2. Add cabbage, green beans, spinach, carrots, and broccoli to the basket. Cover the pot and let it steam until very soft.

3. Once you are done steaming the vegetables, it is time to cook the chicken.

4. Place a pot of water over high heat. When the water starts boiling, place the chicken breasts in the pot and let it cook until the chicken is cooked.

5. Take out the chicken and place it on a cutting board. You can use the cooked chicken water as broth.

6. When the chicken cools down, chop it into small pieces.

7. Cook the rice using the chicken stock. Follow the instructions given on the package of the rice and cook it but use chicken broth instead of water.

8. Transfer the cooked rice to a bowl. Mix well with chicken, oil, steamed vegetables, and some chicken broth.

9. Serve as much as required to your older baby and store the remaining in an airtight container in the refrigerator. It can last for 3 days.

STEW FOR DIABETIC DOGS

Quantity produced: About 15 lb **Preparation time:** 10 minutes **Cooking time:** 50–60 minutes	**Nutritional values for 11.5 oz:** *Calories: 216* *Fat: 3.3 g* *Carbohydrate: 27.6 g* *Protein: 20.1 g*

Ingredients:

- 2 lb dry split chickpeas, rinsed
- ½ lb dried black-eyed peas, rinsed
- ½ lb dried brown lentils, rinsed
- ½ lb dried pearl barley, rinsed
- ½ lb split green peas, rinsed
- ½ lb ground turkey
- 2 ½ lb boneless chicken breasts, cut into ½-inch cubes
- 1 can (14.5 oz) of pumpkin
- 1 lb frozen sliced carrots
- 1 package (10 oz) of frozen chopped spinach
- 1 lb frozen broccoli florets
- 1 lb frozen green beans
- 14 cups water (plus extra for soaking, optional)

Directions:

1. If you have time, soak together the brown lentils, split chickpeas, black-eyed peas, split green peas, and barley in a pot of water for 2–3 hours. If you soak them in water, drain off the water just before cooking.

2. Add water into a large pot. Place the pot over high heat.

3. Add the rinsed brown lentils, split chickpeas, black-eyed peas, split green peas, and barley into the pot. When it starts boiling, turn down the heat to medium and cook covered for about 10 minutes.

4. Stir in the chicken, turkey, pumpkin, carrots, spinach, broccoli, and green beans. Stir occasionally and cook until very little water remains in the pot.

5. Turn the heat off and allow it to sit with the lid on for at least 30 minutes.

6. Let it completely cool down and serve the required quantity.

7. Place some food in an airtight container enough for 3–4 days and place it in the refrigerator.

8. Divide the remaining food into freezer-safe bags (place enough food for 3–4 days in each bag) and freeze.

9. When you require a frozen bag, take out a bag and thaw it for about 10 hours in the refrigerator. Warm the required quantity of food and serve it to your pet.

BEEF AND VEGETABLES FOR DIABETIC DOGS

Quantity produced: About 4–5 lb **Preparation time:** 15 minutes **Cooking time:** 60–80 minutes	**Nutritional values for 16 oz:** *Calories: 630.6* *Fat: 46.6 g* *Carbohydrate: 43.3 g* *Protein: 10.6 g*

Ingredients:

- 1 lb carrots, peeled, sliced, or chopped
- 1 lb celery ribs or zucchini, chopped
- ½ lb sweet potatoes
- 1 ½ lb beef (cheap cuts of mince or chuck and hamburger), chopped
- 2 chicken stock cubes
- ½ lb dried pearl barley, rinsed
- 7–8 cups water

Directions:

1. Add carrots, celery, sweet potatoes, beef, stock cubes, and water into a large pot. You can add roast drippings if desired.

2. Place the pot over high heat. When the water starts boiling, add the pearl barley and stir.

3. Turn down the heat and cook until the barley is tender. Check regularly for water. Add more water if the barley is uncooked and there is no water in the pot.

4. Let it completely cool down. Place enough food in an airtight container sufficient for 3–4 days and place it in the refrigerator.

5. Divide the remaining food into freezer-safe bags (place enough food for 3–4 days in each bag) and freeze.

6. When you require a frozen bag, take out a bag and thaw it for about 10 hours in the refrigerator. Warm the required quantity of food and serve it to your pet.

DIABETIC DOG FOOD WITH VITAMIN THERAPY FOR DOGS REQUIRING INSULIN

(Do not replace this recipe with dog food. Also, do not give more than 2.3 oz for large-breed dogs. Give a smaller quantity for smaller dogs.)

Quantity produced: About 1 ½ lb **Preparation time:** 10 minutes **Cooking time:** 45–50 minutes	**Nutritional values for 2.3 oz vitamin mixture for large dogs:** *Calories: 217.7* *Fat: 21.9 g* *Carbohydrate: 1.4 g* *Protein: 3.7 g*

Ingredients:

For vitamin mixture

- ¾ cup cooked buckwheat groats
- 1 cup water
- ½–1 cup beef liver, sliced
- 1 cup spinach, chopped
- ¼ cup broccoli, finely chopped
- ¼ cup cooked barley
- 1 cup water
- 1 hard-boiled egg, chopped
- ½ cup green beans, chopped
- 2 cups beef, cubed
- ½ tsp garlic, minced

On serving a day (for 1 serving)

- 3 tsp canned pumpkin
- 1 cup (or slightly more) prescription dog food
- ⅓ tbsp cold-pressed wheat germ oil
- ⅓ tbsp brewer's yeast
- 4 oz low-sodium chicken broth

Directions:

1. Preheat the oven to 350 °F.

2. To make the vitamin mixture: All the ingredients in this recipe give some or the other excellent sources of vitamins or minerals, so it is vitamin enriched.

3. Combine beef liver, broccoli, spinach, garlic, green beans, and water in a baking dish and stir. Place it in the oven and set the timer for 20 minutes or until the liver is slightly pink in the middle.

4. Once baked, pour the cooked liquid from the baking dish into a jar. Let it completely cool down and refrigerate until use.

5. Meanwhile, cook the buckwheat groats and barley, following the directions given on the package. Measure out ¾ cup of buckwheat groats and ¼ cup of barley and add into a bowl.

6. Add the baked mixture and egg into a bowl and mix until well incorporated.

7. Transfer into an airtight container and place it in the refrigerator. It can last for 4–5 days.

8. To serve, add about 2.3 oz of the vitamin mixture to the prescription dog food. Mix well with pumpkin, wheat germ oil, brewer's yeast, and chicken broth. The chicken broth to use is the one you have stored in the refrigerator (after baking the beef and vegetables).

9. For smaller dogs, weight divided by 90 will give you the amount of vitamin mixture that should be given.

GRAIN-FREE BEEF AND VEGETABLE MEAL FOR DIABETIC DOGS

Quantity produced: About 2 ½ lb **Preparation time:** 10 minutes **Cooking time:** 10 minutes	**Nutritional values for ½ cup:** *Calories: 52* *Fat: 1.1 g* *Carbohydrate: 4.6 g* *Protein: 6.2 g*

Ingredients:

- ½ lb lean ground beef
- 4 cups fresh green beans, chopped
- 4 cups carrots, chopped
- 1 cup low-fat cottage cheese

Directions:

1. Add beef into a skillet and place it over medium heat. Cook until brown, stirring on and off. Turn off the heat. Discard all the fat from the skillet.

2. Pour enough water in a pot so it is around 2 inches from the bottom up, and place a steamer on it and turn the heat to high.

3. Add green beans and carrots to the basket. Cover the pot and let the vegetable steam until very soft.

4. Let the vegetables cool.

5. Add vegetables into the skillet with the meat. Add cottage cheese and mix well.

6. Serve the required quantity of food and save the remaining in an airtight container. Place the container in the refrigerator. It can last for about 4 days.

FOOD FOR DOGS WITH DIARRHEA AND UPSET STOMACH

Quantity produced: About 2 lb **Preparation time:** 10 minutes **Cooking time:** 20 minutes	**Nutritional values for4 cup:** *Calories: 52* *Fat: 1.1 g* *Carbohydrate: 4.6 g* *Protein: 6.2 g*

Ingredients:

- 1 cup canned pumpkin
- ¼ cup plain yogurt
- 1 cup uncooked white rice
- 2 large boneless, skinless chicken breasts

Directions:

1. Cook the rice following the instructions given on the package.

2. Alongside, place a pot of water over high heat. When the water starts boiling, drop the chicken breasts into the pot. Allow it to boil until the chicken is well cooked.

3. Remove the chicken with a slotted spoon and place it on your cutting board. You can use the cooked chicken water as chicken broth in some other recipes.

4. When the chicken cools down, chop it into small pieces.

5. Transfer the rice to a bowl. Add chicken, yogurt, and pumpkin and mix well.

6. Serve the required quantity to your baby and store the remaining in the refrigerator in an airtight container.

7. Make sure to feed it to your dog within 3–4 days.

HEALTHY HOMEMADE DOG FOOD

(For puppies, adult dogs, diabetic dogs, and senior dogs)

Quantity produced: About 2 lb **Preparation time:** 10 minutes **Cooking time:** 35 minutes	**Nutritional values for 1 cup:** *Calories: 545* *Fat: 13.9 g* *Carbohydrate: 78.4 g* *Protein: 27 g*

Ingredients:

- 1 ½ lb boneless, skinless chicken breasts
- 1 cup yellow squash or zucchini, shredded
- ½ cup frozen green peas, thawed
- 1 ½ cups cooked old-fashioned regular rolled oats
- ½ cup carrots, shredded
- ¼ cup fresh flat-leaf parsley, chopped

Directions:

1. Pour about 2 inches of water into a saucepan and put the chicken into it. The chicken should be covered with water, so add more water if required.

2. Place the saucepan over high heat. When the water starts boiling, turn down the heat to low and let it boil gently until the chicken is cooked.

3. Turn off the heat and cover the saucepan. Let it rest for 30 minutes.

4. Remove chicken from the broth and place it on your cutting board. Do not discard the broth.

5. Cut the chicken into small pieces or the size preferred by your pet.

6. Add chicken, yellow squash, carrots, oats, parsley, and peas into a bowl and mix well.

7. Pour broth into the mixture, a little at a time, and mix well until the desired consistency is achieved.

8. Serve as much as required and place the remaining in an airtight container in the refrigerator. It can last for 3–4 days. You can also place the food in freezer-safe bags and freeze them. This can last for about 3 weeks.

CHICKEN AND QUINOA SOUP

Quantity produced: 3 qt **Preparation time:** 10 minutes **Cooking time:** 35–40 minutes	**Nutritional values for 19 oz:** *Calories: 295* *Fat: 8g* *Carbohydrate: 24.3 g* *Protein: 30.55 g*

Ingredients:

- 2 tbsp coconut oil
- 2 medium zucchinis, chopped
- 3 cups cooked quinoa
- chopped parsley to garnish
- 4 small skinless chicken breasts, cooked, shredded
- 20 baby carrots or 5–6 medium carrots, chopped
- 8 cups water

Directions:

1. Cook quinoa following the directions given on the package. Measure out 3 cups of the quinoa and use it for making soup.

2. Add coconut oil to a stockpot and place it over medium-high heat. When the oil melts, add carrots and stir. Cook until slightly tender.

3. Stir in the zucchini and cook for a couple of minutes. Stir in water and let it come to a boil.

4. Turn down the heat to low. Add chicken and quinoa and stir. Heat thoroughly.

5. Remove the pot from heat and allow the soup to cool down before serving it to your dog. Add parsley and stir.

6. Let the remaining soup cool down to room temperature. Store in the refrigerator in an airtight container. It can last for about 4 days.

7. This soup can be served to puppies, adult, senior, sick, and diabetic dogs.

CHICKEN SOUP

Quantity produced: About 1 ½ qt **Preparation time:** 5 minutes **Cooking time:** 2 hours	**Nutritional values for ½ qt:** *Calories: 199* *Fat: 6.6 g* *Carbohydrate: 22.8 g* *Protein: 12.5 g*

Ingredients:

- 1 potato, peeled, chopped into ½-inch chunks
- 1 stalk celery with leaves, cut into ½-inch pieces
- 2 baby carrots, cut into ½-inch pieces
- 11.5 oz chicken thigh fillets on the bone, trimmed of fat
- a pinch of salt

Directions:

1. Add salt, chicken, potato, celery, and carrots, into a stockpot. Pour enough water to cover the ingredients in the pot.

2. Place the pot over high heat. When the soup starts boiling, turn the heat to low and cook for about 1 ½ hours.

3. Remove any scum or fat that floats on top. Turn off the heat and let it cool down before serving it to your furry baby. Cool the remaining soup completely and store it in an airtight container in the refrigerator. It can last for 3–4 days.

4. This can be served to puppies, adult, senior, and sick dogs.

RAW FOOD CAKES

Quantity produced: 50 balls **Preparation time:** 10 minutes **Cooking time:** 40–45 minutes	**Nutritional values for 1 ball (about 10.2 oz, including cabbage and all the seasoning ingredients):** *Calories: 467* *Fat: 30 g* *Carbohydrate: 37.2 g* *Protein: 22 g*

Ingredients:

- 4 cups brown or white rice
- 8 cups unsalted chicken broth (without onion)
- 4 large yams, cooked
- 4 cups pumpkin puree
- 2 large bunches of parsley, chopped
- 16 large carrots, peeled, chopped into chunks
- 2 cups natural peanut butter
- 1 ⅓ cups nutritional yeast or ⅔ cup dog supplement powder
- 2 cups flaxseeds
- 2 cups raw pumpkin seeds or almonds, ground
- 4 cups rolled oats
- 1 cup olive oil
- 1 cup rose hips, dried, ground
- 2 peaches or pears or 4 plums, pitted or cored
- 2 cups green beans, sliced
- 2 cups snap peas, sliced
- 24 eggshells
- 18 eggs
- 2 heads broccoli, cut into florets
- ½ head cabbage (optional)
- 12 celery stalks, chopped
- 2 large zucchinis or yellow summer squash when in season
- 8 large apples, cored, chopped
- 2 cups cranberries, when in season
- 2 cups blueberries, when in season

Directions:

1. Using cabbage is optional. It can cause a weird smell, so using cabbage is a risk in large quantities. You can try with a smaller quantity and see if your dog will like it.

2. The quantity will reduce when you do not add seasonal ingredients.

3. Grind the flaxseeds in a food processor until finely powdered.

4. The eggshells need to be dry. You can collect eggshells over a few days, and they will dry by the time you prepare. The other option is to place the eggshells on a baking sheet and place it in the oven. Bake for 5–10 minutes or until they are dry. Once dried, powder them in a coffee grinder or spice grinder.

5. Nutritional yeast has a lot of vitamins in it, so it is equivalent to using multivitamin powder.

6. To poach eggs, boil a pan of water over high heat. Turn the heat to medium when the water boils. Stir in about a tablespoon of vinegar.

7. Crack the egg in a bowl. Stir the water using a ladle and carefully slide the egg into the water. Let it simmer for about 2–3 minutes. You will see a film over the yolk; the white will be slightly set.

8. Repeat the previous step for each egg.

9. You should add only one egg into a cup each time, but you can poach 2–3 eggs at a time if your pan is large enough.

10. Remove the egg with a slotted spoon. Hold the spoon over the simmering water to drop off any water from the egg. Place the egg on a plate lined with paper towels.

11. Cook the rice following the directions given on the package. Let the rice cool.

12. You can cook the yams by boiling, roasting, or steaming. Do not remove the peel from the yams. Chop into chunks.

13. Place yams in the food processor and blend until smooth. Transfer into a very large bowl or container.

14. Place carrots, peaches (or any chosen fruit), green beans, snap peas, celery, broccoli, cabbage, zucchini, parsley, apples, blueberries, and cranberries in the blender in batches and process until finely chopped.

15. Transfer the chopped vegetable and fruit mixture into the large bowl with the yam puree. Add cooked rice, flaxseed meal, nutritional yeast or multivitamin powder,

poached eggs, powdered eggshells, oil, pumpkin seeds, pumpkin puree, peanut butter, rolled oats, rose hips, and chicken broth, and give the mixture a good stir using your hands or a large wooden spoon.

16. Line 3–4 baking sheets with parchment paper.

17. Scoop a cupful of the mixture (around 10.2 oz) and drop it on a baking sheet. You can flatten them if desired. Repeat with all the mixture. You should have 50 balls in all.

18. Freeze until firm. Remove the frozen cakes from the baking sheet and place them in freezer-safe bags. You can place sufficient for 2–3 days in the refrigerator and freeze the remaining. For the freezer, make enough bags for 3–4 days.

19. Warm it up before serving. For the frozen cakes, take out the bag from the freezer and thaw for at least 8–9 hours in the refrigerator.

20. This is also suitable for senior and diabetic dogs.

LOW-CARB, HIGH-PROTEIN DOG FOOD

Quantity produced: About 4 lb **Preparation time:** 10 minutes **Cooking time:** 40–45 minutes	**Nutritional values for 6.7 oz:** *Calories: 424* *Fat: 31.1 g* *Carbohydrate: 6.9 g* *Protein: 28.1 g*

Ingredients:

- 1 lb ground turkey
- 1 lb ground beef
- 1 can (7 oz) tuna in water
- 4 oz chicken gizzards
- 2 small eggs
- 3 oz sweet potato
- 3 oz cauliflower florets
- 1 small apple, cored, chopped
- ¼ cup cottage cheese
- ½ cup cooked white rice
- 3 oz cooked green peas
- 3 oz broccoli florets
- 1 ½ tbsp coconut oil

Directions:

1. Boil a pot of water over high heat. Add chicken gizzards into the pot and cook for 10 minutes or until well cooked.

2. Carefully lower the eggs into the pot during the last 5 minutes of cooking. Drain off the water from the pot and let the eggs and gizzards cool down. Once they cool, peel the eggs.

3. Meanwhile, place a large skillet over medium heat. Add ground turkey and beef and stir. Cook until brown and stir occasionally so you break the meat into smaller chunks.

4. Turn off the heat. Retain a little of the cooked fat from the pan and drain off the remaining. Let the meat cool down for a while.

5. Meanwhile, cook the sweet potato in whatever manner (steaming, boiling, roasting, or microwaving).

6. Place peas, cauliflower, broccoli, apple, eggs, and gizzards and process until ground to the desired texture.

7. Transfer the vegetable mixture to a pot. Add tuna and browned beef mixture and mix well.

8. Stir in the coconut oil and cottage cheese. Use as much as required and make portions of the remaining dog food. Transfer the dog food into a freezer-safe bag and freeze. They can last for about a month.

9. To use the frozen food, take a packet from the freezer and thaw it overnight in the refrigerator. Warm it up and serve.

Savory Treats

DIABETIC DOG TREAT

Quantity produced: 4 lb **Preparation time:** 10 minutes **Cooking time:** 25 minutes	**Nutritional values for 2.3 oz:** *Calories: 108* *Fat: 3.72 g* *Carbohydrate: 6.3 g* *Protein: 11.8 g*

Ingredients:

- 1 cup whole wheat flour
- 3 cups beef liver, chopped
- 4 eggs

Directions:

1. Preheat the oven to 350 °F. Place a sheet of parchment paper on a baking sheet.

2. Add beef liver into the food processor bowl and give short pulses until chopped into fine pieces.

3. Add whole wheat flour and eggs and process until smooth and well combined.

4. Spread the mixture on the baking sheet evenly.

5. Place the baking sheet in the oven and set the timer for 15 minutes or until it is firm in the center. It will be soft but firm as well.

6. Cut with a pizza cutter into smaller pieces. Let it cool completely.

7. Transfer into an airtight container and refrigerate until use.

PEANUT BUTTER AND PUMPKIN DOG TREATS

Quantity produced: 50 treats **Preparation time:** 15 minutes **Cooking time:** 40 minutes	**Nutritional values for 1 treat:** *Calories: 55* *Fat: 1 g* *Carbohydrate: 9 g* *Protein: 3 g*

Ingredients:

- 5 cups whole wheat flour
- 1 cup canned pumpkin
- 1 tsp salt
- 2 tsp water or more if required (optional)
- 4 large eggs
- 4 tbsp plain peanut butter
- 1 tsp ground cinnamon

Directions:

1. Preheat the oven to 350 °F. Place a sheet of parchment paper on 2–3 baking sheets.

2. Beat eggs in a bowl. Add pumpkin, salt, peanut butter, and cinnamon and whisk until smooth and well combined.

3. Add flour and mix well.

4. Place the mixture onto your countertop and mix using your hands until the mixture starts sticking together. In case it is not sticking together, add a teaspoon of water at a time and mix well each time. Ensure you add only minimal water, or the treats will be very hard.

5. Divide the dough into 2–3 portions and roll each portion until it is about ½-inch thick. You should get 50 equal pieces.

6. Place them on the baking sheet. Bake in batches.

7. Bake for about 40 minutes or until they are firm and have a crunch in them.

8. Cool completely.

9. Store in airtight containers. You can keep one container at room temperature and store the others in the refrigerator.

10. These treats can be served to diabetic dogs as well.

CHEDDAR DOG TREATS

Quantity produced: 18 treats **Preparation time:** 15 minutes **Cooking time:** 15 minutes	**Nutritional values for 1 treat:** *Calories: 30* *Fat: 1 g* *Carbohydrate: 3 g* *Protein: 1 g*

Ingredients:

- ½ cup all-purpose flour
- ½ tbsp butter, softened
- ½ cup cheddar cheese, shredded
- 3 tbsp whole milk

Directions:

1. Preheat the oven to 350 °F.

2. Add flour and cheddar cheese into a bowl and stir until the cheese is well distributed.

3. Add butter and mix until well combined. Stir in the milk. Mix with your hands until the dough is formed.

4. Dust your countertop with some flour. Place the dough on the dusted part and knead the dough for about a minute.

5. Roll the dough into about a 6 x 4-inch rectangle. Cut into 18 equal pieces and place on a baking sheet. Do not grease the baking sheet.

6. Place the baking sheet in the oven and set the timer for 15 minutes or until they turn golden brown.

7. Once baked, keep the oven door ajar. Let the treats cool completely in the oven itself.

8. Place in an airtight container.

CHICKEN DOG TREATS

Quantity produced: 30 treats **Preparation time:** 15 minutes **Cooking time:** 25 minutes	**Nutritional values for 1 treat:** *Calories: 108* *Fat: 2 g* *Carbohydrate: 17 g* *Protein: 4 g*

Ingredients:

- 4 cups brown rice flour or oat flour
- 1 cup sweet potato, shredded
- 1 cup chicken broth
- 2 cups cooked chicken, shredded
- 2 eggs
- 2 tbsp coconut oil, melted

Directions:

1. Preheat the oven to 350 °F. Place a sheet of parchment paper on a large baking sheet.

2. Add flour, sweet potato, and chicken into a bowl and mix well.

3. Mix in the coconut oil, chicken broth, and eggs until it becomes a smooth dough.

4. Dust some flour on your countertop and place the dough on it and roll with a rolling pin. It should be about ½-inch thick.

5. You can use a bone-shaped cookie cutter or any desired shape of cookie cutter or simply cut the treats into strips with a knife. If you use a cookie cutter, you will be left with scrap dough. Collect the scrap dough and reroll it into a ball.

6. Repeat the rolling, cutting, and rerolling process until all the dough is used up. Using the cooking cutter is a little time-consuming, but it will have a professional touch.

7. Place the treats on the baking sheet. Place the baking sheet in the oven and set the timer for 20–25 minutes or until they turn light golden brown.

8. Cool completely.

9. Store the treats in an airtight container.

CHICKEN JERKY

Quantity produced: 50 jerkies **Preparation time:** 10 minutes **Cooking time:** 2 hours	**Nutritional values for 1 jerky:** *Calories: 30* *Fat: 1 g* *Carbohydrate: 0 g* *Protein: 6 g*

Ingredients:

- 2 lb boneless chicken breasts, cut into ¼-inch slices (preferably skinless)

Directions:

1. Preheat the oven to 275 °F. Place one to two cooling wire racks on a large baking sheet or use two baking sheets if desired.

2. You should have 50 slices of chicken. Place them on the rack.

3. Place the baking sheet in the oven along with the racks. Bake it for 2 hours.

4. Cool completely. Transfer the jerky to an airtight container and place it in the refrigerator. They can last for about 15–20 days.

BACON DOG TREATS

Quantity produced: 30 treats **Preparation time:** 15 minutes **Cooking time:** 15 minutes	**Nutritional values for 1 treat:** *Calories: 103* *Fat: 6 g* *Carbohydrate: 8 g* *Protein: 4 g*

Ingredients:

- 4 slices bacon
- 2 eggs
- ⅔ cup plain natural peanut butter
- 4 tbsp cheddar cheese, shredded
- 2 ripe bananas, peeled, mashed
- 2 tbsp bacon grease
- 2 cups oat flour

Directions:

1. Preheat the oven to 350 °F.

2. Place a pan over medium heat. Add bacon and cook until crisp. Turn off the heat.

3. Remove bacon from the pan with a slotted spoon and place it on a plate. When it cools down, cut it into small bits. Do not discard the bacon grease.

4. Combine banana, eggs, peanut butter, and bacon grease in a bowl.

5. Mix in the oat flour. Once the oat flour is well combined, mix in the cheese and bacon bits.

6. Divide the dough into 30 equal portions and place each in a silicone mold. You can bake them in batches if your molds are not enough. Or you can form them into shapes if you do not want to use the molds.

7. Place the molds in the oven and set the timer for 15–18 minutes.

8. Once baked, let them remain in the molds for about 5 minutes. Remove the treats from the molds and cool them on a wire rack.

9. Store the treats in an airtight container in the refrigerator.

CARROT AND OATS TREAT

Quantity produced: 40 treats **Preparation time:** 10 minutes **Cooking time:** 40 minutes	**Nutritional values for 1 treat:** *Calories: 66* *Fat: 2.1 g* *Carbohydrate: 8 g* *Protein: 3.5 g*

Ingredients:

- 1 cup chicken broth
- 1 cup carrots, finely shredded
- 4 ½ cups oat flour
- 2 eggs
- 4 strips bacon, finely chopped (optional)

Directions:

1. Preheat the oven to 350 °F. Place a sheet of parchment paper on a large baking sheet.

2. Crack the eggs into a bowl. Add chicken broth and whisk until well incorporated.

3. Stir in bacon bits if using carrots.

4. Mix in the flour. Mix with your hands until the dough is formed.

5. Dust some flour on your countertop and place the dough on it and roll with a rolling pin. It should be about ¼-inch thick.

6. You can use a bone-shaped cookie cutter or any desired shape of cookie cutter or simply cut the treats into strips with a knife. If you use a cookie cutter, you will be left with scrap dough. Collect the scrap dough and reroll it into a ball.

7. Repeat the rolling, cutting, and rerolling process until all the dough is used up.

8. Place the treats on the baking sheet. Place the baking sheet in the oven and set the timer for 40 minutes or until they turn light golden brown.

9. Cool completely. Store the treats in an airtight container in the refrigerator.

BASIC DOG BISCUITS

Quantity produced: 6 dozens Preparation time: 10 minutes Cooking time: 25 minutes	Nutritional values for 1 biscuit (without optional ingredients): *Calories: 14.6* *Fat: 0.5 g* *Carbohydrate: 2.1 g* *Protein: 0.4 g*

Ingredients:

- 4 cups all-purpose flour
- 2 cups brewer's yeast
- 2 cups chicken stock
- 1 cup wheat germ
- 6 tbsp canola oil

Optional ingredients (use any)

- bacon bits
- liver powder
- eggs
- cheese, shredded

Directions:

1. Preheat the oven to 400 °F. Place a sheet of parchment paper on one to two large baking sheets.

2. Add flour, brewer's yeast, and wheat germ into a mixing bowl and stir until well combined. If you are using any of the optional ingredients, now is the time to add them.

3. Drizzle oil all over the flour mixture and mix well. Next, add chicken stock and mix until you get a smooth dough. If you use eggs, you will not need all the chicken stock. You may not need it at all. After mixing the eggs, add a little of the stock to form a dough if required.

4. Divide the dough into six equal portions. Shape each portion into a ball.

5. Place a dough ball between your hands and roll it into a log of about ½-inch diameter or whatever thickness you desire. Cut the log into 12 equal slices.

6. Shape each slice into a bone or a bow (hold the slice between your thumb and finger and press along the diameter toward the center). If you do not want to shape them into bones, you can leave them round.

7. Repeat the process with the remaining dough balls (steps 5–8).

8. Place the biscuits on the baking sheets. Bake them in batches.

9. Bake for 20–25 minutes or until done. Once baked, keep the oven door ajar. Let the biscuits cool completely in the oven for about 2 hours.

10. Place the biscuits in an airtight container in the refrigerator.

11. You can make the biscuits using whole wheat or oat flour.

VEGAN DOG BISCUITS

Quantity produced: About 1 lb **Preparation time:** 15 minutes **Cooking time:** 15 minutes	**Nutritional values for the entire batch:** *Calories: 998* *Fat: 10 g* *Carbohydrate: 196 g* *Protein: 32 g*

Ingredients:

- 1 cup carrot puree
- ¼ tsp ground cinnamon
- ⅔ cup oat flour
- ⅔ cup whole wheat flour
- ⅔ cup all-purpose flour

Directions:

1. Preheat the oven to 400 °F.

2. Combine oat flour, whole wheat flour, all-purpose flour, and cinnamon in a mixing bowl.

3. Stir in the carrot puree using your hands and mix into a smooth dough.

4. If the dough is very dry and crumbling apart, add more carrot puree or a little water. If the dough is sticky, add a little flour and mix until smooth.

5. Divide the dough into two portions. Shape them into balls.

6. Place two sheets of parchment paper on your countertop. Dust each sheet with some flour.

7. Place a dough ball on each sheet and roll with a rolling pin until it is about ½-inch thick.

8. Cut into biscuits of desired size and shape. Lift the parchment paper and the biscuits and place each on a baking sheet. You can cut the biscuits into different shapes using a cookie cutter. If you are using a cookie cutter, collect the scrap dough. Form into a ball once again and repeat the process of making the biscuits until all the biscuits are made.

9. Bake in batches for 15 minutes per batch or until they turn crisp.

10. Cool completely and transfer into an airtight container. Place the container in the refrigerator.

CHICKEN, RICE, AND CHEESE DOG TREAT

Quantity produced: 20 treats **Preparation time:** 10 minutes **Cooking time:** 45 minutes	**Nutritional values for 1 treat:** *Calories: 62* *Fat: 3.1 g* *Carbohydrate: 3.5 g* *Protein: 4.5 g*

Ingredients:

- 2 cups cooked chicken chunks, chopped
- ½ cup cheese, shredded
- ⅔–1 cup low-fat, low-sodium chicken stock
- 2 cups cooked white rice
- 6 tbsp white rice flour
- 2 tbsp dried basil or cilantro

Directions:

1. Preheat the oven to 400 °F. Place a parchment or wax paper on the bottom of a large baking pan.

2. Add rice and chicken to the food processor bowl. Add a little of the chicken stock and process until well combined. Add more stock, a little at a time, and process each time until you get a thick paste. You may not require all of the stock.

3. Add cheese and rice flour and process until well combined.

4. Spread it into a baking dish. Mark lightly the treats into squares of about 1 inch or 20 equal slices using a knife or pizza cutter.

5. Set the oven timer for 45 minutes and place the baking dish in the oven. For softer treats, take out the baking dish and cut the treats fully (on the lightly marked area). Let them cool.

6. If your dog prefers crunchy treats, turn the biscuits over and continue baking for another 30–40 minutes or longer, if required, until crunchy.

7. Transfer the treats into an airtight container when they are cooled down completely. Place the treats in the refrigerator.

8. You can also place them in freezer-safe bags and freeze them. They can last for about 3 months.

Homemade Kibble

CHICKEN AND VEGETABLE KIBBLE

Quantity produced: About 20 cups **Preparation time:** 25 minutes **Cooking time:** 3 hours	**Nutritional values for ½ cup:** *Calories: 90* *Fat: 2.3 g* *Carbohydrate: 8 g* *Protein: 9 g*

Ingredients:

- 8 cups cooked chicken
- 4 cups cooked sweet potato
- 2 cups cooked green beans
- 4 tbsp olive oil
- 4 cups cooked carrots
- 1–2 cups flour

Directions:

1. Preheat the oven to 400 °F. Place a sheet of parchment paper on one to two large baking sheets.

2. Place chicken and oil into the food processor bowl. Process until smooth.

3. Transfer the chicken to a large mixing bowl.

4. Add about a cup of flour and mix well. If you find the dough sticky, add more flour, about 2 tbsp at a time, and mix well each time. You may not require all the flour.

5. Divide the dough into two portions. Place each portion on a prepared baking sheet.

6. Roll the dough with a rolling pin until you get the desired thickness. Cut lightly to the desired size with a knife or a pizza cutter.

7. Place the baking sheets in the oven on two racks and bake for 2–3 hours or until brown and firm to the touch. Interchange the baking sheets every 30–40 minutes to bake evenly.

8. Cool completely on your countertop. Break into pieces along the marked part.

9. Transfer the cooled kibbles into an airtight container and refrigerate. They can last for about a week.

MULTIGRAIN KIBBLE

Quantity produced: About 4 ½–5 lb **Preparation time:** 10 minutes **Cooking time:** 45 minutes	**Nutritional values for 6.5 oz:** *Calories: 337* *Fat: 6.5 g* *Carbohydrate: 60.4 g* *Protein: 15.9 g*

Ingredients:

- 4 cups whole wheat flour
- 1 cup soy flour
- 2 cups nonfat dry powdered milk
- 1 cup wheat germ
- 2 tbsp salt
- 3 tbsp corn oil or any other cooking oil
- 3 cups all-purpose unbleached flour
- 2 cups cornmeal
- 2 cups rolled oats

- 1 cup brewer's yeast
- 2 large eggs
- 3–6 cups water

Directions:

1. Preheat the oven to 350 °F.

2. Crack and whisk the eggs into a bowl. Add oil and whisk some more.

3. Combine whole wheat flour, soy flour, powdered milk, wheat germ, salt, cornmeal, rolled oats, and brewer's yeast in a large mixing bowl.

4. Add about 3 cups of water and mix well.

5. Add the egg–oil mixture and whisk until smooth. You should have a thin batter like a pancake. So add more water if required.

6. Divide the batter in two to three large rimmed baking sheets. The batter should be around ½ inch, so use baking sheets accordingly.

7. Bake in batches for around 45 minutes or until light brown around the edges.

8. Break into small pieces.

9. You can store them in an airtight container in the refrigerator or freezer-safe bags in the freezer. The frozen ones can last you for about a month, and the refrigerated ones can last for about 10 days.

NUTTY PUMPKIN KIBBLE

Quantity produced: About 2 ½–3 lb **Preparation time:** 15 minutes **Cooking time:** 35 minutes	**Nutritional values for 1.5 oz:** *Calories: 138* *Fat: 3.9 g* *Carbohydrate: 21.6 g* *Protein: 6 g*

This is suitable for all dogs, especially those with digestive problems and diabetes.)

Ingredients:

- 2 cans of pumpkin puree
- 1 cup oats
- 6 tbsp natural peanut butter
- 4 eggs
- 6 cups whole wheat flour, brown rice flour, or gluten-free flour
- 1 tsp ground cinnamon (optional)

Directions:

1. Preheat the oven to 350 °F.

2. Mix oats, whole wheat flour, and cinnamon in a large mixing bowl.

3. Crack the eggs into a bowl. Add pumpkin puree and peanut butter and whisk until smooth.

4. Pour the egg mixture into the bowl of the flour mixture and stir until well combined and smooth dough is formed.

5. Dust your countertop with some flour. Dust your hands and the rolling pin as well and place the dough on the countertop.

6. Roll the dough until it is about ½ inch in thickness.

7. Cut into pieces, or if you want to give shape to the kibbles, use any cookie cutter you prefer.

8. Place the kibbles on two to three large baking sheets and bake in batches until golden brown. It may take around 30 minutes.

9. Cool the kibbles completely on cooling racks.

10. You can store them in an airtight container in the refrigerator or freezer-safe bags in the freezer. The frozen ones can last you for about a month, and the refrigerated ones can last for about 10 days.

APPLE AND VEGETABLE KIBBLE

Quantity produced: Around 8 lb **Preparation time:** 15 minutes **Cooking time:** 90 minutes per batch	**Nutritional values for 6 oz:** *Calories: 182* *Fat: 7.1 g* *Carbohydrate: 21.2 g* *Protein: 10.35 g*

Ingredients:

- 2 ⅛ cups brown rice
- 10 cups water
- 2 medium sweet potatoes, scrubbed, chopped
- 1 ½ cups steel-cut oats
- 4 small sprigs of rosemary, finely chopped
- ½ cup olive oil, canola oil, or sunflower oil (plus extra to grease)
- 1 cup lentils
- 6 medium carrots, peeled, chopped
- 2 apples, peeled, cored, chopped, or 1 cup of unsweetened applesauce
- 2 ½ tbsp fresh parsley, minced
- 2.2 lb ground turkey

Directions:

1. Grease three to four baking sheets with some oil and set aside.

2. Heat a saucepan over medium heat and add rice and lentils to it. Pour 7–8 cups of water over the lentils to cover them.

3. When it boils, turn down the heat and simmer until cooked. Add some more water if required.

4. Add sweet potatoes, carrots, apples, oats, and fresh herbs, and cook for 20–25 minutes. Add more water if your mixture feels dry. Turn off the heat and let it cool for 10–15 minutes.

5. In the meantime, place a skillet over medium heat. Add turkey and cook until brown. Stir often. As you stir, crumble the meat. Turn off the heat and cool for 10–15 minutes.

6. Preheat the oven to 350 °F.

7. Add half the turkey and half the rice mixture into the food processor bowl and process until smooth. Spread the blended mixture on a prepared baking sheet.

8. Repeat the previous step.

9. Bake in batches for about 45 minutes, flipping sides halfway through baking. Remove from the oven and cool. You can also place two baking sheets in the oven on different racks but make sure to interchange the place of the baking sheets every 20 minutes or so.

10. When cool enough to handle, chop the kibbles into smaller pieces.

11. Spread it back on the baking sheets.

12. Lower the oven temperature to 325 °F and bake for about 50 minutes or until cooked. They need to dry thoroughly, or else, they can get moldy after a few days. Remove from the oven and cool completely.

13. Refrigerate in an airtight container until use. It should last for about 10 days when stored properly.

CRUNCHY KIBBLE

Quantity produced: About 3 ½ lb (without optional ingredients) **Preparation time:** 15 minutes **Cooking time:** 45 minutes per batch	**Nutritional values for 3.9 oz:** *Calories: 276* *Fat: 7.1 g* *Carbohydrate: 42.5 g* *Protein: 9.3 g*

Ingredients:

- 12 cups whole wheat flour or oat flour
- 2 cups powdered milk
- 5 cups broth, water, or milk
- 6 large eggs or 8 medium eggs
- ⅔ cup canola oil, olive oil, or cooking oil of your choice

Optional (use any)

- 2–3 cups meat, shredded
- 2–3 cups vegetables, shredded
- 1–2 cups cheese, shredded
- 2–3 cups fruit puree or fruit, finely chopped

Directions:

1. Preheat the oven to 350 °F.

2. Spray cooking spray on two to three large baking trays.

3. Combine flour and powdered milk in a bowl using a wooden spoon.

4. Add eggs, oil, and broth into another bowl and whisk with a wooden spoon.

5. Pour the egg mixture into the flour mixture and mix well. If you are using any optional ingredients, now is the time to add them to the flour, and mix well.

6. If the mixture is very dry, add some more broth; if it is sticky, add more flour. Divide the mixture onto the prepared baking sheets.

7. Spread the mixture evenly until 1 ½ inches thick. Bake in batches, for around 45 minutes or until done. You can place two baking sheets in the oven on different racks and bake. Interchange the racks halfway through baking.

8. Remove from the oven and cool. Break into pieces.

9. Transfer into an airtight container or freezer-safe bag. Refrigerate or freeze until use. It can last for a week in the refrigerator or 3 months in the freezer.

DRY DOG FOOD WITH BEEF AND VEGETABLES

Quantity produced: About 1 ½ lb **Preparation time:** 10 minutes **Cooking time:** 30 minutes	**Nutritional values for 6.4 oz:** *Calories: 365* *Fat: 17.4 g* *Carbohydrate: 32.8 g* *Protein: 20.9 g*

Ingredients:

- ½ lb lean ground beef
- 1 ½ cups whole wheat flour
- 1 egg
- 1 tbsp Worcestershire sauce
- ½ cup carrots, finely chopped
- ½ cup beans, finely chopped
- ½ tsp coconut oil
- ½ cup dry milk
- ¼ cup vegetable oil
- ¾ cup low-sodium beef broth

Directions:

1. Melt coconut oil in a pan and place the pan over medium heat. When the oil melts, add beef and cook until brown. As you stir, break the meat into smaller crumbles. Take the pan off the heat. Let it cool until the vegetables steam.

2. Place a pot over high heat and pour 2 inches of water in it.

3. Place a steamer basket in the pot. Place the carrots and beans in the basket. Cover the pot. When it starts boiling, turn down the heat to medium-low and steam the vegetables for about 10 minutes or until tender. Remove the vegetables and let them cool for a few minutes.

4. Add flour and dry milk into a bowl and stir until well incorporated.

5. Crack the egg into a bowl. Add vegetable oil, broth, and Worcestershire sauce and whisk well.

6. Pour the egg mixture into the bowl of flour. Also, add the beef and the steamed vegetables and mix well. The dough will be somewhat sticky and chunky as well, which is perfectly okay.

7. Preheat the oven to 350 °F.

8. Coat a rimmed baking sheet with cooking spray. Place the mixture on the baking sheet and spread it evenly until it is about ½-inch thick.

9. Remove the baking sheet from the oven and cut it into bite-size pieces with the help of a knife or pizza cutter.

10. Cool completely.

11. Transfer the kibbles into an airtight container or freezer-safe bag. Refrigerate or freeze until use. It can last for a week in the refrigerator or a month in the freezer.

DRY VEGAN DOG FOOD

Quantity produced: About 3 lb Preparation time: 15 minutes Cooking time: 2 hours	Nutritional values for 2.7 oz: *Calories: 195* *Fat: 4.4 g* *Carbohydrate: 29.7 g* *Protein: 9.9 g*

Ingredients:

- 1 cup dried pinto beans
- ½ large sweet potato, scrubbed, chopped
- ½ cup lettuce
- 1 tbsp peanut butter
- 1 cup brown rice
- ½ large carrot, chopped
- 1 tbsp flaxseeds
- ½ tbsp coconut oil

Directions:

1. Follow the directions given on the packages of the rice and dried beans and cook them.

2. Add the cooked beans, rice, carrot, potato, and flaxseeds into a pot.

3. Add 1–2 cups of the cooked beans' water and cook until the vegetables are soft. Add more of the cooked water if required.

4. Turn off the heat and let it cool completely. Transfer the ingredients to a food processor and process until smooth.

5. Preheat the oven to 350 °F.

6. Melt the coconut oil to grease a large rimmed baking sheet.

7. Pour the blended mixture on the baking sheet and spread it thinly.

8. Place the baking sheet in the oven and set the timer for 45 minutes.

9. Now, take out the baking sheet and flip the sides. Bring the oven's heat to 300 °F and continue baking for 45 minutes.

10. Take the baking sheet from the oven and bring the temperature down to 200 °F.

11. Let it cool for a few minutes. Break the kibbles into pieces. Place the baking sheet in the oven once again and bake for about 30 minutes or until they are dried completely.

12. Cool them down completely.

13. Transfer the kibbles into an airtight container or freezer-safe bag. Refrigerate or freeze until use. It can last for a week in the refrigerator.

DRY DOG FOOD WITH TURKEY AND VEGETABLES

Quantity produced: About 2 lb **Preparation time:** 10–15 minutes **Cooking time:** 45–60 minutes	**Nutritional values for 4.3 oz (without fish oil):** *Calories: 356* *Fat: 20.45 g* *Carbohydrate: 14.7 g* *Protein: 26.8 g*

Ingredients:

- 4 cups carrots or pumpkin, chopped
- 4 eggs
- 2 lb boneless and skinless turkey or chicken
- ⅔ cup plain yogurt
- 1–2 cups all-purpose flour (or more if required)
- 4–5 fish oil capsules (optional)

Directions:

1. Place chicken, carrots, eggs, and yogurt in the food processor and process until smooth. Cut off the tip of the fish oil capsules and squeeze the oil into the food processor.

2. Add about ½ cup of flour and process until well combined. You should be able to roll the mixture, so add flour accordingly.

3. Grease two to three rimmed baking sheets with some oil.

4. Spread the mixture on the baking sheets. Cut into pieces of the desired size.

5. Preheat the oven to 200 °F. Bake in batches for about an hour or until nice and dry.

6. Separate the pieces and cool completely. Transfer the kibbles into an airtight container in the refrigerator. You can store them in freezer-safe bags in the freezer. They can last for about a month.

Sweet Treats

PEANUT BUTTER PUPCAKES

Quantity produced: 1 dozen **Preparation time:** 15 minutes **Cooking time:** 20 minutes	**Nutritional values for 1 pupcake:** *Calories: 106* *Fat: 6 g* *Carbohydrate: 10 g* *Protein: 2 g*

Ingredients:

For the cupcakes

- 4 tbsp natural peanut butter
- 2 medium bananas, peeled, mashed
- 1 cup flour
- ½ tsp baking powder
- 1 tsp baking soda
- 4 tbsp cooking oil
- 4 tbsp honey

For the frosting

- 4 oz cream cheese
- 4 tbsp natural peanut butter
- 1 medium banana, peeled, mashed

Directions:

1. Preheat the oven to 350 °F.

2. Grease a muffin pan of 12 counts with a cooking spray. Place disposable liners in each.

3. To make the cupcakes, add peanut butter, mashed banana, oil, and honey into a bowl and whisk until smooth.

4. Combine flour, baking powder, and baking soda in another bowl and stir well.

5. Add the flour mixture into the bowl of the banana mixture. Stir until smooth.

6. Divide equally and spoon the batter into the cups of the muffin pan.

7. Place the muffin pan in the oven and set the timer for about 18–20 minutes or until brown on the outside and cooked through inside.

8. The toothpick test: Insert a toothpick in the middle of a cupcake and take it out. If you find any batter stuck on the toothpick, you need to bake them for a few more minutes.

9. Cool the cupcakes in the pan itself for about 5 minutes. Take the cupcakes out and place them on a wire rack to cool to room temperature.

10. To make the frosting, whisk together peanut butter, cream cheese, and banana in a bowl.

11. Spoon the frosting into a piping bag and pipe the frosting over the cupcakes. You can use only peanut butter and cream cheese or peanut butter and banana for the frosting.

12. Place cupcakes in an airtight container in the refrigerator.

BLUEBERRY DOGGY MUFFINS

Quantity produced: 12 mini muffins **Preparation time:** 10 minutes **Cooking time:** 15 minutes	**Nutritional values for 1 mini muffin:** *Calories: 67* *Fat: 3.2 g* *Carbohydrate: 9.5 g* *Protein: 1.1 g*

Ingredients:

- ½ cup whole wheat flour
- a tiny pinch of salt
- 3 tbsp honey
- ½ cup frozen blueberries (do not defrost)
- ½ tsp baking powder
- 2 tbsp melted coconut oil
- ⅛ cup milk of your choice

For blueberry icing

- 2 tsp frozen blueberries (do not thaw)
- ¼ cup sour cream or Greek yogurt

Directions:

1. Preheat the oven to 375 °F. Grease a mini muffin pan (12 counts) with cooking oil spray. Place disposable liners in each of the 12 cavities.

2. Add baking powder, flour, and salt into a mixing bowl and stir until well combined.

3. Stir in honey, coconut oil, and milk. Stir until just combined. Do not overmix.

4. Add blueberries and fold gently.

5. Divide the batter into the prepared muffin pan. Place the pan in the oven and set the timer for 15–18 minutes or until golden brown on top and cooked through inside. To check if it is cooked inside, check the previous recipe for the toothpick test.

6. Cool the mini muffins in the pan itself for about 5 minutes. Remove them from the pan and place them on a wire rack to cool to room temperature.

7. To make the frosting, combine sour cream and blueberries in a bowl.

8. Spoon the frosting over the muffins and serve. Store the remaining muffins in an airtight container in the refrigerator.

FROSTY PEANUT BUTTER POPSICLES

Quantity produced: About 2 ⅓ cups **Preparation time:** 5 minutes plus freezing time **Cooking time:** 0 minutes	**Nutritional values for the entire batch:** *Calories: 1,572* *Fat: 101.9 g* *Carbohydrate: 108.3 g* *Protein: 78.8 g*

Ingredients:

- 1 cup smooth peanut butter, sweetened
- ½ cup low-fat yogurt
- ⅔ cup water (or more if required)

Directions:

1. Ensure the peanut butter is not sweetened by xylitol or other artificial sweeteners.

2. Place peanut butter, yogurt, and water in a blender until smooth. If it is not pourable, add more water and blend.

3. Pour the blended mixture into ice cube trays. Freeze until firm.

4. Remove the Popsicle cubes from the tray and place them in a freezer-safe bag or container in the freezer.

STRAWBERRY AND BANANA DOG ICE CREAM

Quantity produced: 40–45 oz **Preparation time:** 10 minutes plus freezing time **Cooking time:** 0 minutes	**Nutritional values for the entire batch:** *Calories: 621* *Fat: 3.7 g* *Carbohydrate: 92.8 g* *Protein: 62 g*

Ingredients:

- 20 medium strawberries
- 20 oz natural plain yogurt
- 2 medium ripe bananas, sliced

Directions:

1. Place the strawberries in a bowl and mash with a potato masher until you get small pieces.

2. Add bananas and mash until the texture your doggy would prefer is achieved.

3. Add yogurt and mix until well combined.

4. Spoon into ice cube trays and freeze until firm. These can last for about 2 months.

5. From the ice trays, you can transfer the ice cream into a freezer-safe bag and freeze it.

PEANUT BUTTER AND BANANA ICE CREAM

Quantity produced: About 3 ½ cups **Preparation time:** 10 minutes plus freezing time **Cooking time:** 0 minutes	**Nutritional values for the entire batch:** *Calories: 1,247* *Fat: 80 g* *Carbohydrate: 102.9 g* *Protein: 49.4 g*

Ingredients:

- 2 ripe bananas, peeled, sliced
- ½ cup sweetened peanut butter
- 16 oz plain low-fat yogurt

Directions:

1. Blend the bananas, peanut butter, and yogurt until smooth.

2. Spoon into ice cube trays and freeze until firm. These can last for about 2 months.

3. Transfer the ice cream to a freezer-safe bag and freeze.

Meals and Pastries for Special Occasions

RABBIT MEAL

Quantity produced: 40–45 oz Preparation time: 10 minutes plus freezing time Cooking time: 0 minutes	Nutritional values for 1 cup: *Calories: 461* *Fat: 1.7 g* *Carbohydrate: 4.1 g* *Protein: 3.7 g*

Ingredients:

- 1 rabbit (about 2 lb)
- 1 cup barley
- 4 cups water
- ¼ cup wild rice
- ¼ cup asparagus, chopped
- ¼ cup carrots, chopped
- ¼ cup kale, chopped
- ¼ cup lima beans
- 1 small potato, chopped
- ½ cup plain yogurt
- 3 tbsp canola oil

Directions:

1. Place the rabbit in a pot of water over high heat. When the water starts boiling, turn down the heat and cover the pot. Cook until the rabbit is well cooked and comes off the bones.

2. Remove the rabbit with a slotted spoon and place it on your cutting board. Take off all the bones from the rabbit and the pot and discard them.

3. Add the rabbit meat back into the pot.

4. Stir in the wild rice, barley, lima beans, potato, asparagus, carrots, and kale. Cover the pot and cook until the grains are tender and hardly any broth is left in the pot.

5. Turn off the heat. Add canola oil and mix well. Add yogurt and stir.

6. Serve. You can store the leftover meal in an airtight container in the refrigerator.

BEEF STEW

Quantity produced: 3 cups Preparation time: 10 minutes Cooking time: 30 minutes	Nutritional values for 1 cup: *Calories: 217* *Fat: 9 g* *Carbohydrate: 15 g* *Protein: 20 g*

Ingredients:

- ½ lb beef stew meat, cut into bite chunks
- ½ carrot, peeled, cut into 1-inch cubes
- 1 tbsp coconut oil
- ½ sweet potato, peeled, cut into 1-inch cubes
- ½ broccoli, cut into bite-size florets

Directions:

1. Add coconut oil into a saucepan and let it melt over medium heat.

2. Once the oil melts, add beef and stir. Cook for a few minutes until it no longer looks pink.

3. Stir in the sweet potato, carrot, and broccoli. Stir for a couple of minutes.

4. Add water and stir. Cover the saucepan and cook on low heat until the meat and vegetables are cooked.

5. Cool to the desired temperature and serve.

SHEPHERD'S PIE FOR DOGS

Quantity produced: 6 mini pies
Preparation time: 20 minutes
Cooking time: 20 minutes

Nutritional values for 1 mini pie:
Calories: 207
Fat: 14.1 g
Carbohydrate: 6 g
Protein: 14.2 g

Ingredients:

- ½ lb ground beef
- ¼ cup sweet peas, chopped or pureed
- ⅛ tsp garlic powder
- 1 small egg, lightly beaten
- ¼ cup cheese, shredded
- ¼ cup carrots, chopped or pureed
- ¼ cup plain breadcrumbs
- ½ tsp parsley
- ⅔ cup cooked mashed potatoes

Directions:

1. Preheat the oven to 375 °F.

2. Add beef, sweet peas, parsley, carrot, breadcrumbs, and egg into a bowl and mix until well combined.

3. Divide the mixture equally and scoop the mixture into 6 muffin cups. Do not grease the muffin cups. Line them with disposable liners if desired.

4. You can use leftover mashed potatoes or make some using instant mashed potatoes according to the instructions given on the package.

5. Transfer the mashed potatoes into a piping bag and pipe it over the meat mixture.

6. Place the muffin cups in the oven and bake for about 20 minutes or until the meat mixture is cooked.

7. Let the pies cool down before you serve them.

DOG BIRTHDAY CAKE

Quantity produced: 1 cake with 10 slices Preparation time: 15 minutes Cooking time: 25 minutes	Nutritional values for 1 slice: *Calories: 157* *Fat: 6 g* *Carbohydrate: 20 g* *Protein: 4 g*

Ingredients:

For the birthday cake

- 1 egg
- 2 tbsp canola oil or vegetable oil
- 3 tbsp honey or maple syrup
- 1 cup whole wheat flour
- ¼ cup peanut butter (natural or regular but xylitol-free)
- ⅓ cup milk or water

- 1 ¼ cups carrots, shredded
- 1 ¼ tsp baking soda

For the fluffy frosting

- ½ cup plain yogurt or water
- 10–11 oz potatoes, peeled, chopped into chunks

Directions:

1. To make the cake, preheat the oven to 350 °F. Grease two round small baking pans (about 4–5 inches in diameter) with oil. Line them with parchment paper as well.

2. Crack the egg into a bowl. Add oil, milk, peanut butter, and honey and whisk until smooth.

3. Add carrots and stir in the baking soda and flour. Stir until just combined, making sure not to overmix.

4. Distribute the batter among the baking pans and spread the batter evenly.

5. Place the baking pans in the oven and bake for about 20 minutes or until done (do the toothpick test; refer to the *Peanut Butter Pupcakes* recipe).

6. Let them cool in the pans for 10 minutes. Remove the cakes from the pans and cool them on a wire rack.

7. Meanwhile, make the frosting. Cook the potatoes in a pot of boiling water (or you can steam or microwave them) until soft.

8. Place the cooked potatoes in a bowl. Add yogurt and beat with an electric hand mixer set over medium speed until light and creamy.

9. Place one cake on a plate or a cake stand. Spread about ¼ of the frosting over the cake. Place the other cake on top of this cake. Spread the remaining frosting on top and sides of the cake.

10. You can decorate with sprinkles or small dog treats or biscuits if desired.

MINI PUMPKIN PIE

Quantity produced: 6	Nutritional values for 1 pie:
Preparation time: 15 minutes	*Calories: 86*
Cooking time: 45 minutes	*Fat: 2 g*
	Carbohydrate: 15 g
	Protein: 3 g

Ingredients:

For the pie crust

- 1 small egg
- 6 tbsp oat flour

For the pumpkin filling

- ½ can (from 15 oz can) of pure pumpkin puree

- ½ tbsp honey
- 1 small egg
- ¼ tsp ground cinnamon

For the whipped cream topping

- ¼ cup plain low-fat Greek yogurt
- 1–2 tsp low-fat or 2% milk
- ¼ cup cornstarch (optional, to achieve stiff peaks)
- ¼ tsp ground cinnamon

Directions:

1. Preheat the oven to 350 °F.

2. To make the pie crust, place oat flour in a bowl. Add egg and mix until you get a smooth dough.

3. Roll the dough on your countertop with a rolling pin. Cut the dough into smaller rounds (you may get three or four) with a cookie cutter to fit into six mini pie pans.

4. Collect the scrap dough, repeat the previous step once or twice, and get the remaining crusts, six in all.

5. Place a crust in each mini pie pan. Press it well onto the bottom as well as the sides. You can use the last batch of scrap dough and press it around the sides of the pie pans.

6. Place the pie pans in the oven and set the timer for 8 minutes.

7. To make the filling, crack the egg into a bowl. Add pumpkin puree, cinnamon, and honey and beat with an electric hand mixer until smooth. Spoon the mixture over the crusts.

8. Place the crust in the oven and continue baking for 25–30 minutes.

9. Meanwhile, prepare the whipped cream topping. Place Greek yogurt in a bowl. Add milk and cornstarch and whip until smooth.

10. Spoon the topping over the filling on the pie. Garnish each with cinnamon and serve.

CHAPTER 7: IMPERIAL AND METRIC CONVERSION CHART

Imperial	Metric
1 in.	2.54 cm
1 oz	28.3 g
1 lb	453 g
2.2 lb	1 kg
1 fl oz	29.57 ml
1 cup	236.6 ml
F = C x (9/5) + 32 (convert to Fahrenheit)	C = (F – 32) x 5/9 (convert to Celsius)

CONCLUSION

Thank you for making it to the end of this guide. I hope you have learned much about feeding your dog healthy and wholesome meals. When you have a loyal companion, it can be very rewarding to put in a little extra effort and cook them homemade meals just like any other person in your family.

Commercial dog foods are never as healthy as they claim to be. The best nutritious choice is picking the right ingredients and cooking good food for your dog. Homemade dog food is especially beneficial for dogs with allergies, sensitivities, and gastrointestinal issues. By picking the healthiest ingredients yourself, you can ensure your dog is not consuming anything that might harm its health.

All the recipes in this book are tried and tested by dog owners from all over. You can try them out to see what suits your dog the best. Remember to keep rotating meals and avoid feeding the same food too long. This will help ensure that your dog is fed a variety of vitamins, minerals, and other nutrients needed to maintain good health.

So start trying these recipes and cook healthy, delicious homemade meals for your dog!

REFERENCES

Bovender, T. (n.d.). *Healthy dog stew*. Just a Pinch Recipes. https://www.justapinch.com/recipes/main-course/other-main-course/healthy-dog-stew-comfort-food-for-your-fido.html

Braff, D. (2016, October 13). *Common mistakes humans make cooking dog food*. Ollie. https://blog.myollie.com/common-mistakes-humans-make-cooking-dog-food/

Brown, D. (2022, May 18). *How to feed dogs with food allergies and hypersensitivity*. Top Dog Tips. https://topdogtips.com/feed-dogs-with-food-allergies/

Deb. (2021, November 19). *DIY vegan dog food*. A Vital Yopp! http://www.avitalyopp.com/recipe/diy-vegan-dog-food/

Different diets for dogs. (2021, December 14). Bow Wow Meow Pet Insurance. https://bowwowinsurance.com.au/pet-community/pet-talk/different-diets-for-dogs/

dish567. (2022, September 13). *Homemade dog food with beef*. Allrecipes. https://www.allrecipes.com/recipe/275423/homemade-dog-food-with-beef/

Giovanelli, N. (2020, September 29). *Dog food allergies - Nutritional management*. The Canine Health Nut. https://thecaninehealthnut.com/dog-food-allergies/

How much should I feed my dog? Calculator and feeding guidelines. (n.d.). Doodle Doods. https://doodledoods.com/how-much-should-i-feed-my-dog-calculator/

Kearl, M. (2019, October 31). *Cooking for your dog: Pros and cons of cooking homemade dog food*. American Kennel Club. https://www.akc.org/expert-advice/nutrition/cooking-for-your-dog-dos-and-donts/

Kmac1805. (n.d.). *Chicken balls (for dogs) recipe*. Food. https://www.food.com/recipe/chicken-balls-for-dogs-385731

Park, A. (2022, February 7). *Homemade puppy food recipes: Vet-approved*. Top Dog Tips. https://topdogtips.com/homemade-puppy-food-recipes/

77 ingredient suggestions for balanced home made dog food. (n.d.). Daily Dog Stuff. https://www.dailydogstuff.com/nutritious-ingredients-list-for-home-made-dog-food/

The Ohio State University Veterinary Medical Center. (n.d.) *Basic calorie calculator for dogs and cats*. https://vet.osu.edu/vmc/companion/our-services/nutrition-support-service/basic-calorie-calculator

Toxic food for dogs. (n.d.). Battersea. https://www.battersea.org.uk/pet-advice/dog-care-advice/toxic-food-dogs

Verlinden, A., Hesta, M., Millet, S., & Janssens, G. P. J. (2007, January 18). Food allergy in dogs and cats: A review. *Critical Reviews in Food Science and Nutrition*, *46*(3), 259–273. https://doi.org/10.1080/10408390591001117

Image References

anialaurman. (2018, June 26). *Dog eating veggies* [Image]. Pixabay. https://pixabay.com/photos/cherries-cherry-set-child-village-3497780/

annmariephotography. (2019, September 18). *Dog cake* [Image]. Pixabay. https://pixabay.com/photos/puppy-dog-birthday-celebrate-4484296/

BarkingRoyalty. (2022, July 16). *Dog kibble* [Image]. Pixabay. https://pixabay.com/photos/dry-dog-food-dog-food-dog-kibble-7336506/

Coulton, M. (2020, May 15). *Kibble* [Image]. Pixabay. https://pixabay.com/photos/dog-food-dog-bowl-dog-kibble-5168940/

Coulton, M. (2020, May 18). *Wet food* [Image]. Pixabay. https://pixabay.com/photos/dog-food-dog-bowl-wet-dog-food-5175604/

Dan, D. (2021, February 16). *Kibble* [Image]. Pixabay. https://pixabay.com/photos/pet-food-pet-food-dog-cat-6018384/

Hein, R. (2021, February 13). *Beef and veg stew* [Image]. Pixabay. https://pixabay.com/photos/soup-stew-food-healthy-6008222/

Hudgins, L. (2015, November 16). *Dog treat cupcakes* [Image]. Pixabay. https://pixabay.com/photos/dog-treats-cupcakes-fancy-party-1021396/

jagdprinzessin. (2017, September 2). *Food as per size* [Image]. Pixabay. https://pixabay.com/photos/golden-retriever-puppy-2706672/

Julita. (2020, April 25). *Dog walking* [Image]. Pixabay. https://pixabay.com/photos/grass-meadow-plants-wind-walk-5088100/

Michele. (2015, August 19). *Dog eating bone* [Image]. Pixabay. https://pixabay.com/photos/dog-bone-ostrich-hungry-eating-889991/

nutmarketca. (2011, April 12). *Pumpkin pie* [Image]. Pixabay. https://pixabay.com/photos/pumpkin-pie-food-delicious-1323131/

Raphael. (2018, February 19). *Dog treats* [Image]. Pixabay. https://pixabay.com/photos/treats-delicious-dog-bone-dog-food-3164687/

Scholz, R. (2020, November 18). *Dog owner* [Image]. Pixabay. https://pixabay.com/photos/dog-pet-pet-owner-animal-owner-5753302/

spoba. (2019, September 2). *Dog eating veggies* [Image]. Pixabay. https://pixabay.com/photos/carrot-vegetables-vitamins-food-4445193/

Willimann, L. (2017). *Dog eating* [Image]. Pixabay. https://pixabay.com/photos/dog-meal-food-bowl-dog-food-feed-2210717/

Made in the USA
Las Vegas, NV
02 March 2024

86629545R00059